PROTECT YOUR MONEY

PROTECT YOUR MONEY

Lyle Allen

CeShore

Pittsburgh, Pa

ISBN 1-58501-000-6

Trade Paperback
© Copyright 1999 Lyle Allen
All rights reserved
First Printing—2000
Library of Congress #98-87016

Request for information should be addressed to:

CeShore Publishing
The Sterling Building
440 Friday Road
Pittsburgh, PA 15209
www.ceshore.com

Cover design: Michelle Vennare - SterlingHouse Publisher
Typesetting: AJ Rodgers - SterlingHouse Publisher

CeShore is an imprint of SterlingHouse Publsher, Inc.

Printed in Canada

CONTENTS

TABLE OF CONTENTS

INTRODUCTION

How would you like to retire with no financial worries? You can if you make plans for your retirement and take advantage of investment opportunities.

Where will your retirement money come from? Probably from a company retirement plan or Social Security. Don't think these programs will cover all your expenses when you retire. They will provide only about 50 percent of what you'll need. That means, if you want to retain your current standard of living, you'll need investments to supplement your retirement income.

One thing to remember is that the retirement picture in America is undergoing a gradual and probably permanent change. Both government and private industry have become more stingy toward retirees in recent years. What's more, many companies are dropping their defined-benefit retirement plans and replacing them with employee 401(K) and other defined-contribution plans. These changes will place more responsibility on you for your retirement.

This book will show you how to map out a retirement plan, avoid costly mistakes, and maximize your retirement income. Best of all, it will show you how to take advantage of the investment opportunities that mutual funds provide for retirement. The book is divided into four parts, and each is designed to provide the tools you'll need for a comfortable retirement.

Part 1 takes a hard look at Social Security as well as other types of retirement plans, and points out their advantages and disadvantages. It examines the mechanics of retirement plans, provides information about the options that the various plans offer, and supplies you with a menu of investment choices for your retirement dollars.

In Part 2, you'll learn about the many types of mutual funds, the basics of investing in them, how they work, and how to choose a fund that's right for you. Furthermore, you'll learn how to invest in mutual funds using the DCAP formula. This easy-to-use formula is a successful investment strategy that can help you realize a good return when you invest in funds. The formula is a long-term investment strategy that requires regular investments according to a predetermined target price. The DCAP formula has the potential to make your retirement years free of financial worry. In addition to mutual funds, Part 2 includes other types of investments. Thus, you can decide which ones are best to meet all your retirement needs. In a very real sense, you'll learn how to create your own investment portfolio.

Part 3 first explains how to look objectively at your family's finances, and suggests several ways to reduce your living expenses. Then it shows you how to start a savings plan. When you save part of your income, you gain control of your financial future. You'll learn that a savings plan requires organization, application, and management. A prosperous retirement rests on your ability to save money.

There's more to retirement planning than just putting aside money. You'll need to ensure that your estate passes on to your heirs. So in Part 3, you'll learn how to integrate wills, trusts, insurance, and retirement benefits into an estate plan. Only when a retirement plan is a part of your estate can you use its benefits most effectively.

The do's and don'ts of planning and investing for retirement are listed in Part 4. This includes 25 basic rules for creating your own retirement lifestyle. In addition, there is a question and answer chapter that examines many of the topics discussed in this book.

If you already have a retirement plan, this book offers helpful advice that could increase your retirement income. If you don't have a plan, it will show you how to start one. Regardless of when you plan to retire, your income, or your age, this book can get you started on a prosperous retirement.

This book is intended for people of all ages whose goal is to build and preserve a retirement free of financial worry. If that's your goal, let's look at Social Security in Chapter 1.

Part One
RETIREMENT PLANS

...but will a man content
himself with a handful of dried
peas? He is born to be rich.

–Ralph Waldo Emerson

Chapter 1

SOCIAL SECURITY

If you are like many people, Social Security is probably the first thing you think about when it comes to retirement. Unfortunately, Social Security won't cover all of your financial needs when you retire. It is intended only to supplement a company pension, savings, annuities, and other investments.

The Social Security program, enacted into law in 1935, is the basic retirement program of most working Americans. The idea behind Social Security is that you pay taxes into the system when you work, and you or your family receive benefits when you retire or should you become disabled. In addition, your survivors could receive benefits when you are deceased.

In the 1970s and early 1980s, the Social Security system faced serious financial problems. These problems were resolved and the system is more sound, at least until early into the next century when the future of Social Security is uncertain.

Social Security benefits are provided under four programs:

> * The Old-Age and Survivors Trust Fund — for retirees, their families, and the families of deceased workers.

> * The Disability Insurance Trust Fund — for disabled workers and their families.

> * Medicare — an insurance program that provides benefits under the Hospital Insurance Trust Fund.

> * Supplemental Security Income (SSI) — for people with low income and few assets. This program is administered by Social Security but financed from general revenues of the U.S. Treasury.

Here is a description of the four Social Security programs and the benefits that could be available to you.

RETIREMENT BENEFITS

Qualifying for benefits

The amount of your Social Security retirement benefits depends on factors such as your age, the type of benefit you receive, and the amount of your earnings. If you contribute to Social Security, you'll probably earn more credits than you need to qualify for benefits. These extra credits won't increase your benefits, but the additional income you receive from working will boost your benefits.

You can apply for reduced retirement benefits at age 62 and full benefits at 65. To be eligible for benefits, you need 40 credits or 10 years of work. You can earn credits by working and paying Social Security taxes, known as FICA (Federal Insurance Contributions Act) on most income statements.

If you were born before 1938, you will be eligible for full benefits at age 65. However, beginning in the year 2000, the age for full benefits increases from 65 to 67.

Amount of benefits

If you receive Social Security retirement benefits at age 62, they are reduced by 5/9 of one percent for each month you receive them before age 65. Thus, you get 80 percent of your primary insurance amount (PIA) at age 62. At age 65, you receive 100 percent of your PIA. The closer you are to 65 when you receive benefits, the larger the benefits will be. Social Security benefits automatically increase with the Consumer Price Index (CPI).

If you delay the receipt of your Social Security past age 65, your benefits can increase in two ways. First, your extra income probably will increase your average earnings, the basis for determining the amount of your benefits. Second, you receive a special credit for delaying your benefits. The credit, which is a percent added to your Social Security benefits, varies depending on your date of birth. The rate gradually increases to eight percent per year for people turning age 65 in the year 2008.

The table on the opposite page (Table 1-1) provides an estimate of monthly Social Security retirement benefits.

Additional information

You can receive a free Personal Earnings and Benefit Estimate Statement (Form SSA-7004) by contacting: Social Security Administration, P.O. Box 20, Wilkes-Barre, PA 18711-2030, toll-free telephone number: 800-937-2000. The statement shows your Social Security earnings history and estimates how much you have paid in Social Security taxes.

DISABILITY BENEFITS

Social Security's definition of disability is generally related to a physical or mental condition that prevents you from working for at least a year. The program is not intended for a temporary condition or partial disability, and differs from private

ESTIMATED AVERAGE MONTHLY SOCIAL SECURITY BENEFITS
Before and After the December 1999
Cost of Living Adjustment (COLA)

	Before 2.4%COLA	After 2.4% COLA
All retired workers	$785	$804
Aged Couples		
Both Recieving Benefits	$1,316	$1,348
Widowed Monther and Two Children	$1,573	$1,611
Aged Widow(er) Alone	$757	$775
Disabled Worker, Spouse		
and One or More Children	$1,225	$1,255
All Disabled Workers	$736	$754

Table 1-1

programs and those of other government agencies. So if you qualify for disability benefits from another source, you may not be eligible for disability under Social Security.

You must have worked long enough and recently under Social Security to qualify for disability benefits. Your eligibility also depends on your age when you become disabled and the number of work credits you have earned. You can earn a maximum of four work credits each year. Generally, you need 20 credits earned within the last 10 years for eligibility.

Family benefits

If you are eligible for disability (or retirement) benefits, other members of your family also could be eligible for benefits. This means benefits could be paid to:

* Your wife or husband if your spouse is age 62 or older.

* Your wife or husband if your spouse is caring for your child who is under age 16 or disabled.

* Your children if they are unmarried and:

– Under age 18.

– Under age 19 and enrolled full-time in an elementary or secondary school.

– Over age 18 but severely disabled before age 22.

A family member benefit is usually equal to fifty percent of your disability payment. For example, your spouse if over age 65 is eligible to receive fifty percent. The payment is reduced for each month your spouse is under 65 to age 62.

Amount of benefits

The monthly amount of your disability benefits will depend on your lifetime average earnings covered by Social Security. To receive an estimate of your disability benefits, contact Social Security and request a copy of your Personal Earnings and Benefit Estimate Statement.

Extent of benefits

You can receive disability benefits until your condition improves or you return to "substantial" employment. Your claim is periodically checked to determine your condition and there are special Social Security regulations such as working without the sudden loss of benefits if you return to work.

For more information on disability benefits, contact a Social Security office for a free copy of Publication 05-10029, Disability.

MEDICARE

The Medicare program helps pay for the health care costs of people over age 65 and many disabled people. Although Medicare can pay for a large part of your health costs, it does not cover all your expenses. There are some expenses that you must pay.

Medicare has two parts: Part A is a hospital insurance program financed by your Social Security taxes, and Part B is medical insurance paid by participants and the federal government.

Part A

Part A helps pay for inpatient hospital care and limited follow-up medical care. Anyone aged 65 (and eligible for Social Security or railroad retirement) is automatically eligible for Medicare Part A. You also may qualify on a spouse's Social Security record. In addition, you are covered under Part A for permanent kidney failure that requires dialysis or a kidney replacement.

Part B

Part B is voluntary and helps pay for doctors' services, outpatient hospital care, and other medical care. If you are eligible for hospital insurance under Part A, you are probably eligible to enroll in the Part B medical insurance program. The monthly premium for the Part B insurance is deducted from your Social Security benefits.

How to receive Medicare benefits

If you are receiving Social Security benefits, you are automatically enrolled under Part A of Medicare at age 65. But you have the opportunity to refuse Part B. Should you continue working after age 65 and don't enroll in Social Security, you can still enroll in Medicare.

If you are disabled, you are automatically enrolled in Medicare after you receive disability benefits for 24 months. Again, you have the opportunity to refuse Part B.

SUPPLEMENTAL SECURITY INCOME (SSI)

The SSI program is administered by Social Security, but not financed by Social Security taxes or Social Security trust funds. To receive SSI payments, you must have a low income and few assets. In addition, you must meet the following requirements:

> * Be a U.S. citizen, or legally living in the U.S., or the Northern Mariana Islands.

> * Be age 65 or older, blind, or disabled.

SSI payments for low income takes into account the money you receive from Social Security, retirement plans, and other sources. The value of non-cash items such as free housing and food are considered income.

Assets that are considered to determine SSI eligibility include your property, cash, and savings. Assets not considered include your house, many personal belongings, and usually your auto.

The amount you'll receive from SSI depends on your income and where you live. The basic monthly SSI benefit is the same for all states. But some states add their own funds to supplement the basic benefit.

If you need more information about the SSI program, contact Social Security and request a free copy of SSI publication No. 05-11000.

OTHER BENEFITS

Other Social Security benefits are available when certain requirements are met. These benefits include:

> * Benefits for divorced people.

> * Survivors benefits.

> * A one-time death benefit.

> * Benefits to divorced widows and widowers.

SOCIAL SECURITY AND EMPLOYMENT

There is a limit to the amount of money you can earn under Social Security and continue to receive full benefits. The limit affects people under age 70 who receive retirement, dependent, or survivor benefits.

If you are under 65, you can earn up to $8,640 (for 1997) and still receive full Social Security benefits. For every $2 you earn over the limit, $1 is withheld from your benefits.

If you are age 65 to 69, you can earn up to $13,500 (for 1997) and still receive full benefits. For every $3 you earn over the limit, $1 is withheld from your Social Security benefits.

TAXABLE BENEFITS

Once you start receiving Social Security, you may have to pay federal income taxes on a portion of your benefits. The tax threshold is between $25,000 and $34,000 for individuals and between $32,000 and $44,000 for couples filing jointly.

1993 tax law changes

Under the Omnibus Budget Reconciliation Act of 1993, you could pay higher federal taxes on your Social Security benefits if unmarried and your income exceeds the limit of $34,000 or married filing jointly with income over $44,000. Before 1993, under the old tax law, up to 50 percent of your benefits were subject to taxes if they exceeded the limit. With the new tax law that took effect January 1994, up to 85 percent of your benefits are now subject to taxes.

Figuring your Social Security taxes

To determine whether you have to pay taxes on your Social Security benefits, add one-half of your benefits to your other income (including tax-exempt income less adjustments for IRAs, Keoghs, and alimony). If you are unmarried and the total is under $25,000 or married filing jointly and the total is under $32,000, there is no tax on your benefits.

If you are unmarried with total income over $25,000 but less than $34,000, or married filing jointly with total income over $32,000 but less than $44,000, you are taxed on 50 percent of your benefits.

If you are unmarried with a total income over $34,000 or married filing jointly with total income over $44,000, the 1993 tax law created a new threshold of benefit inclusions. When benefits are over $34,000 for singles or $44,000 for couples, 85 percent of that portion over the new threshold up to $4,500 for singles or $6,000 for couples is subject to tax. The smaller of that total or 85 percent is taxable.

Information source

You can receive additional information on taxes and your Social Security benefits by requesting Publication 554, Tax Benefits for Older Americans, and Publication 915, Tax Information on Social Security, from the Internal Revenue Service (IRS).

SELF-EMPLOYMENT

If you are self-employed and your net income is over $400 for the year, you must report the earnings for Social Security tax and credit purposes. As a self-employed person you'll receive a quarter of Social Security coverage for each $670 of income (for 1997), up to a maximum of four quarters of coverage. If you have both taxable wages and self-employment income, your wages receive credit for Social Security benefits first. Then, the amount of your self-employment income needed to raise earnings to the taxable maximum is subject to the self-employment tax.

The amount of your self-employment tax is based on your net self-employment income from all sources. The tax totals 15.3 percent: 12.4 percent Social Security tax and 2.9 percent Medicare tax. For 1993, the Social Security portion of the tax applies to a maximum of $57,600 income and the Medicare portion to a maximum of $135,000 income.

HOW TO APPLY FOR SOCIAL SECURITY BENEFITS

You can apply for benefits at any Social Security office or call Social Security's toll-free number, 800-234-5772.

Some of the documents you need for Social Security to determine whether you are eligible and the amount of your benefits include:

* Your Social Security card (or Social Security number).
* Your birth certificate.
* Marriage certificate (if you enroll on a spouse's record).
* Your most recent W-2 Form or your latest tax return if you are self-employed.

SOCIAL SECURITY PUBLICATIONS

There are several publications that cover the Social Security programs. You can receive a free catalog, SSA Publication No. 05-10036, that describes these programs by contacting:

> Social Security Administration
> Office of Public Affairs
> Public Information Distribution
> Center
> P.O. 17743
> Baltimore, MD 21235
> Telephone: (410) 965- 0945
> Fax number: (410) 965- 0696
> www.ssa.gov on the WEB

Chapter 2
TYPES OF RETIREMENT PLANS

If you were planning a vacation, you wouldn't wait until you were away from home to decide where to go. The same reasoning should apply to your retirement. You should plan for retirement years before you leave your job. In fact, every stage of your life — from your first to your last job — requires different planning strategies to assure you'll have enough money to retire in comfort.

Contrary to what some people believe, companies are not required to provide their workers with a retirement plan. As it turns out, most companies do have retirement plans to attract new workers and to reward loyal employees.

There are several types of retirement plans, but they all have a basic ingredient — to allow you to save for your retirement. Your plan, whether it is a 401(K), profit-sharing, Keogh, or another type, will provide the base for your retirement income.

If you don't participate in a retirement plan where you work, maybe it's time to start. And it's usually up to you rather than your employer to initiate your participation. If you do have a plan, it's to your benefit to understand how it works. Do you know, for example, whether the contributions to your retirement plan are tax deductible? Are you vested in your plan? Do you know your plan's payout options? These are some of the questions this chapter and the following ones will answer for you.

PENSIONS AND RETIREMENT PLANS

Although the terms pension and retirement plan are often used interchangeably, there is a difference. A pension is a payment, not wages, that is made regularly to a retiree or retiree's family. It is paid because the retiree has fulfilled conditions of employment and is, therefore, entitled to a pension. A retirement plan is used in a broader context and includes all types of retirement plans, including pensions. In most cases, this book uses the term retirement plan, even when pension might be more appropriate.

Retirement plans are grouped in two categories: private and public. A private retirement plan is nongovernment and includes commercial, industrial, service, educational, and charitable organizations. A public retirement plan covers employees of federal, state, and local government, the police, government-owned corporations, and similar groups.

UNDERSTANDING RETIREMENT PLANS

There are two basic types of private retirement plans: defined-benefit and defined-contribution. The main difference between the two types is that under a defined-benefit plan your employer saves and invests a fixed amount for your retirement, while your employer usually offers you a choice of investments if you have a defined-contribution plan.

Defined-Benefit Plans

If you have a defined-benefit plan, your employer sets aside money for your retirement and decides the amount you will receive when you retire. The amount is determined by a formula that is usually based on your salary, how long you worked for your employer, and whether your benefits are adjusted for inflation. The amount you receive in retirement could be as high as the average of your three highest consecutive years of salary. Here are some points to remember about defined-benefit plans:

> * Many defined-benefit plans are paid in the form of an annuity with equal payments over your lifetime. Others provide you the option to receive a lump-sum payment at retirement.

> * Usually, defined-benefit plans don't include cost of living adjustments for inflation.

> * Your employer must offer you a "qualified joint and survivor annuity." This means that after you die your spouse is entitled to at least 50 percent of the amount you were receiving in retirement.

> * Defined-benefit plans are eligible for insurance coverage by the Pension Benefit Guaranty Corporation (PBGC), a quasi-government organization that guarantees vested pension benefits.

Defined-contribution plans

The most significant retirement change in recent years has been a shift from defined-benefit to defined-contribution retirement plans. Defined-contribution plans total more than 80 percent of all company retirement plans.

If you have a defined-contribution plan, your employer may (but is not required to) make contributions to your plan. The amount your employer can contribute is up to 25 percent of your annual income, but not over $30,000 in any one year. An advantage of a defined-contribution plan is that it offers you more tax savings than a defined-benefit plan. This is because you contribute most of the money to a defined-contribution plan.

The potential value of a defined-contribution plan depends mainly on the investment choices your employer offers and the selections you make. Many employers offer a broad range of choices from growth stock funds and money market funds to company stock and profit-sharing. Defined-contribution plans are not eligible for insurance coverage by the PBGC.

401(K) PLANS

The 401(K) is the most popular and fastest growing of all retirement plans. It is a defined-contribution plan that offers you an active role in managing your retirement money. You can contribute to a 401(K) if your employer has adopted one and you meet the plan's eligibility requirements.

There are several names for 401(K) plans. Sometimes a 401(K) is called a "retirement income fund," "retirement plan," or simply "savings plan." Whatever the name, these plans are established under Section 401(K) of the Internal Revenue Service Code.

You can contribute to a 401(K) plan through payroll deductions. However, there is a limit to the salary reduction contributions you can make to your 401(K). For 1997, the limit was $9,500.

Your employer may contribute to your 401(K) whether or not you contribute, or your employer may match your contributions on a dollar-for-dollar basis or as a percentage of your contributions. Your contributions grow tax-deferred until you withdraw the money.

Summary plan description

If you have a 401(K), your company is required to provide you with a summary plan description that explains the rules of your plan. Since this is the main reference for information about your 401(K), you should check regularly with the retirement benefits office where you work to ensure your summary plan description is up to date.

Investment choices

A 401(K) plan could offer you up to six investment choices. The choices might include: stock, bond, and balanced mutual funds; guaranteed investment contracts; your company's stock; and money market funds.

Switching among investments

The summary plan description states whether you may switch among the investments offered in your 401(K). Most plans not only allow you to select your investments but also to switch among them. However, many 401(K) plans have restrictions on how often you can switch from one investment to another.

Vesting

Vesting is the right to receive your employer's contributions to your 401(K) should you change jobs before retirement. Your contributions to a 401(K) are always 100 percent vested. Your employer's contributions are vested over a period of years according to the vesting standards of the Employee Retirement Income Security Act(ERISA).

Each year that you work for your employer you become more vested in your 401(K) plan. Usually, after 5 to 7 years of work with the same employer, you are fully vested. This means that you will receive 100 percent of your retirement benefits should you leave your employer or retire.

Leaving your employer before retirement

If you leave your employer before you are eligible to retire, any lump-sum distribution from your 401(K) could be subject to a 20 percent federal withholding tax, unless you rollover your money directly into another 401(K) or individual retirement account (IRA) within 60 days.

There are two types of rollovers: direct and indirect. A direct rollover is accomplished with a trustee (person or institution handling your account) to trustee transfer of your account. An indirect rollover, where you actually receive the money and then reinvest it, exposes you to the federal withholding tax. Although if you are assessed the 20 percent tax, you can claim a refund when you file your income taxes.

Retirement distributions

You can start receiving distributions from your 401(K) plan at age 59 and 1/2 and distributions must begin by age 70 and 1/2. Many 401(K) plans provide the option to receive distributions as a lump sum; an annuity over a period of years; or a rollover into an IRA. If you are under age 70 and 1/2, it may be possible to leave your money in your 401(K) even after you retire.

Withdrawing and borrowing money

Under certain circumstances, most 401(K) plans allow you to withdraw your contributions before age 59 and 1/2. If you have a hardship, for example, you may be allowed to withdraw money from your 401(K). A hardship is defined as immediate and heavy financial need such as high medical expenses or education costs. To qualify for a hardship withdrawal, you'll have to prove that the money you need is not available from other sources.

In addition to a hardship withdrawal, your 401(K) plan may allow you to borrow from your account. Many 401(K) plans allow participants to borrow as much as one-half of the balance in their account, up to a maximum of $50,000.

Most 401(K) loans are subject to a 5-year repayment rule. Any remaining balance beyond the five-year period is considered a distribution which exposes you to an early withdrawal penalty and taxes. The best way to repay a 401(K) loan is probably by payroll deduction. This method protects you against an early withdrawal penalty and taxes.

Annual statement

You will receive an annual statement from your employer that shows your 401(K) investments and whether you have a vested right to receive them. It's a good idea to compare the rate (percent) of return on your investments against other investment choices in your 401(K) plan. If your return is less than what other investments provide, it might be wise to switch investments.

SIMPLIFIED EMPLOYEE PENSION-INDIVIDUAL RETIREMENT ACCOUNT (SEP-IRA)

A SEP-IRA is both a pension plan and a type of IRA. If you are a self-employed person, you can establish a SEP-IRA regardless of whether or not you have any employees. The requirements to establish a SEP-IRA are similar to other qualified retirement plans.

A SEP-IRA provides a way to lower your adjusted gross income (AGI) and maximize your retirement savings. You can contribute 15 percent of your taxable income up to $24,000 to a SEP-IRA. Your contributions are tax-deferred until you start withdrawing them, and the amount of your contributions are indexed annually for inflation.

TAX-SHELTERED ANNUITY (TSA)

A tax-sheltered annuity, Section 403(b) of the Tax Code, is a retirement plan offered by public schools and tax-exempt organizations. There are two types of TSA plans. Under one type of plan, your employer makes tax-deferred contributions to your TSA. The contributions are not subject to Social Security or Medicare deductions.

Under the other type of plan, you agree with your employer to take a salary reduction or forego a salary increase in exchange for your employer's contribution to your TSA. The contributions are tax-deferred but subject to Social Security and Medicare deductions.

Your contribution to a TSA cannot exceed the lower of 25 percent of your yearly income or $30,000. If your employer also contributes to your TSA, the combined contributions cannot exceed 25 percent of your yearly income or $30,000, whichever is lower. You must make all of your TSA contributions through payroll deductions. Other TSA rules include the following:

> * You can change the amount of your contribution only once each year. However, you can stop your contribution at any time.
>
> * You may borrow as little as $500 or as much as $50,000 from your annuity, tax-free (subject to IRS rules), at a low interest rate.
>
> * At all times, you are 100 percent vested.
>
> * If you leave your job, your TSA contributions can remain with your employer or be rolled over into an IRA.
>
> * There is no early withdrawal penalty for these TSA distributions:

–Because you are disabled.

–If you receive equal payments (at any age) and you plan to
   deplete your TSA over your life expectancy.

–After you reach age 55 and become separated from service.

–To your beneficiary in case of your death.

* Distributions must begin by age 70 1/2 and they are taxed as
ordinary income.

PROFIT-SHARING PLAN

A profit-sharing plan requires a company to contribute a portion of its year-end profits into a fund for employees. The maximum contribution to a profit-sharing account cannot exceed 15 percent of an employee's annual compensation, with a limit of $30,000. As an employee, you don't have to contribute to a profit-sharing plan. A profit-sharing plan usually offers you the choice to invest in your company's stock, mutual funds, and fixed-income securities. In addition to profit-sharing, your employer may offer you another type of retirement plan such as a 401(K). Profit-sharing plans are not covered by the PBGC.

EMPLOYEE STOCK OWNERSHIP PLAN

An Employee Stock Ownership Plan (ESOP) is a defined-contribution plan, similar to a profit-sharing plan. If you participate in an ESOP, your company contributes shares of its stock to a trust account held in your name.

In addition to your employer's contribution, many ESOP plans will allow you to buy additional shares of company stock. The maximum yearly contribution you and your employer can make to an ESOP is 25 percent of your salary up to $30,000.

ESOP advantages

If you participate in an ESOP, you can accumulate company stock at little or no cost and become a company owner. Additionally, you can achieve full vestment after 5 or 7 years, and you have the choice to rollover your ESOP to an IRA if you leave the company.

ESOP disadvantages

An ESOP can be a good retirement plan if your company makes sufficient contributions to your account and its stock appreciates in price. However, there is no guarantee that the stock's price will go up.

Since an ESOP holds, almost exclusively, company stock it could be a high risk investment. An economic downturn, stock market drop, or decrease in the company's earnings could reduce the value of your ESOP. Thus, it makes sense to limit your contributions to an ESOP to no more than 25 percent of your total retirement account.

Diversification

If you participate in an ESOP for at least ten years, at age 55 you can request that 20 percent of your plan's assets be in investments other than your company's stock. At age 60, fifty percent can be in noncompany investments. It's important to diversify your ESOP account as you near retirement age so your retirement won't be entirely dependent on your company's stock.

TARGET-BENEFIT PLAN

A target-benefit plan is based on the amount you need to accumulate a fund sufficient to provide you a certain income at retirement age. If you are an older worker or a manager and your employer wants to make maximum contributions to your retirement, it may offer you a target-benefit plan.

A target-benefit plan is similar to a defined-contribution plan in that contributions cannot be over a certain percentage of your income. It's also similar to a defined-benefit plan because distributions are set in advance, before you retire.

KEOGH PLAN

If you earn self-employed income, you may be eligible for a Keogh plan. You can contribute to a Keogh plan if you're in business for yourself, whether it's part-time or full-time. Many types of organizations can set up a Keogh plan, including:

* Sole proprietorships.

* Partnerships.

* Subchapter S corporations.

* Limited liability companies.

* Incorporated businesses.

If you establish a Keogh plan for yourself, you must make contributions to Keogh plans for your full-time employees. Your contributions are a tax-deductible business expense.

There are two types of Keogh plans: defined-contribution and defined-benefit. Both allow you to set aside money for your retirement.

Defined-contribution Keogh

A defined-contribution Keogh plan is a money-purchase or profit-sharing plan. For 1998, the plan allowed you to make annual contributions up to 25 percent of your net income or a maximum of $30,000 to a Keogh. For 1998, the maximum net earnings or wages that can be taken into account in figuring the contribution and the deductions for contributions is $160,000. Once you decide your percentage contribution, you must continue with that percentage whether or not your company is profitable.

The benefits you receive at retirement depend on such factors as the amount of your contributions, investment earnings, and the plan's expenses. Your contributions are not taxable until you withdraw them.

Defined-benefit Keogh

A defined-benefit Keogh plan is designed to produce a predetermined amount of retirement income. There is no yearly limitation on the amount of your contributions to a defined-benefit plan, but there is a limit on the yearly amount of benefits you can receive under the plan. For 1998, the annual benefits you can receive from a defined-benefit plan cannot exceed the lower of $130,000 or the average of your highest three consecutive years' net profits.

Keogh rules

Like other retirement plans, there are rules that you must follow if you establish a Keogh plan.

* If you have full-time employees, they are eligible to participate in a Keogh after 1 year of employment and they must be fully vested in 7 years. As an alternative, you could require that employees work 2 years before they participate in a Keogh, but after that period all future contributions are fully vested.

* Part-time employees (those working less than 1,000 hours a year) and those under age 21 may be excluded from a Keogh.

* Withdrawals from a Keogh before age 59 and 1/2 are subject to penalty and taxes.

* If you become disabled before age 59 and 1/2, you can withdraw your Keogh money without penalty.

* You must start distributions from your Keogh by age 70 and 1/2.

* You can receive distributions in a lump sum, installments, or in an annuity. All withdrawals are taxed as ordinary income.

* If you are no longer self-employed, you can roll over your Keogh account to another qualified retirement plan.

For more information on Keogh plans, call the IRS at 800-Tax-Form and request IRS Publication 560, Self-employment Retirement Plans.

Savings Incentive Match Plan For Employees

A Savings Incentive Match Plan for Employees (SIMPLE) is a retirement plan for small employers. The provisions of this plan allow employers to establish a SIMPLE for qualified employees as part of a 401(K) or individual retirement account (IRA).

Under a SIMPLE plan, an employer is required to do the following:

> Match an employee's contribution to the plan on a dollar-for-dollar basis up to 3 percent of the employee's compensation. The 3 percent contribution may be reduced to not less than 1 percent of an employee's compensation for no more than two out of any five years; or make a 2 percent contribution to eligible employees' accounts under the plan, regardless of whether or not employees contribute to the plan.

> Your contributions to a SIMPLE are based on a percent of your compensation and cannot exceed $6,000 per year (1998), an amount that is indexed for inflation. In addition, your contributions are excluded from your income, and your earnings are tax deferred. Distributions from a SIMPLE plan are taxed under the rules for IRA distributions.

> Early withdrawals from a SIMPLE account are generally subject to a 10 percent penalty, but a 25 percent penalty applies to withdrawals made during the first two years under the plan.

State And Local Retirement Plans

Unlike private retirement plans covered under ERISA, public retirement plans for state and local government employees are exempt from federal regulations.

The retirement benefits of most state and local employees are defined-benefit plans and paid in the form of an annuity. About 10 percent of state and local employees have both defined-benefit and defined-contribution plans.

In general, state and local pension plans are comparable to those provided by private plans. However, public plans usually provide higher benefit amounts than private retirement plans. Also, a larger percentage of public plan recipients receive greater post-retirement increases.

Federal Retirement Plans — Civilian Employees

Civilian employees (non-military) are covered under one of two plans: the Civil Service Retirement System (CSRS) or Federal Employee Retirement System (FERS).

FERS became effective January 1, 1987, and covers most federal employees who were hired, or rehired, following a break in service of more than one year after January 1, 1984, and other employees who choose to transfer to FERS.

FERS is a newer and more flexible retirement plan than CSRS. For example, FERS employees are covered by Social Security while CSRS employees are not covered. Thus, FERS employees can build two retirement plans at the same time. Both plans require employees to contribute a percentage of their pre-tax income to their retirement.

In addition to their regular retirement plan, federal employees can contribute to a Thrift Savings Plan. This plan offers employees the opportunity to contribute a percent of their base pay to tax-deferred investments.

Creditable military service

Generally, active military service is counted towards government retirement if it ended under honorable conditions. Military service includes service in the Army, Navy, Air Force, Marine Corps, Coast Guard, service academies, the Regular or Reserve Corps of the Public Health Service (after June 30, 1960), and as a commissioned officer of the National Oceanic and Atmospheric Administration (after June 30, 1961).

Disability retirement

Disability retirement requires employees to have at least five years of creditable government service and be unable to perform their work because of disease or injury.

Retirement annuity

Government retirement plans seldom pay benefits in a lump sum. Instead, they are distributed as an annuity similar to those paid by an insurance company, but employees' benefits are guaranteed by the government, not an insurance company.

The amount of a government annuity depends mainly on an employee's years of service and high-three salary years. Usually, at age 55 with 30 years of service, employees receive about 56 percent of their average high-three salary years. The maximum annuity is 80 percent of the average high-three salary years.

Cost of living adjustment

Government annuities include a cost of living adjustment (COLA) for employees and their annuity survivors. COLA increases are determined by the percent of increase in the average Consumer Price Index (CPI) for the "base quarter" (July through September) of the effective year over the "base quarter" of the preceding year.

Social Security

Federal employees may receive both a government retirement annuity and Social Security benefits, provided they qualify for both. Social Security benefits do not reduce the amount of a government annuity.

FEDERAL RETIREMENT PLAN — MILITARY PERSONNEL

The retirement benefits of military personnel depend on the dates of service. Those who entered the military before August 1, 1986, can retire after 20 years of service with 50 percent of pay.

For each year from 20 to 30 years, the amount increases until it reaches a cap of 75 percent of base pay.

Military personnel who entered the service after August 1, 1986, receive 40 percent of their base pay after 20 years of service and 75 percent after 30 years.

Military retirement also provides benefits to surviving spouses if they were married to an eligible retiree for 1 year. Spouses receive about 55 percent of the retirement benefit.

Chapter 3
INDIVIDUAL RETIREMENT ACCOUNTS

An Individual Retirement Account (IRA) is an almost perfect investment for retirement. The advantages of an IRA are that you are not only saving for retirement but you are deferring taxes in your peak earning years.

If you have taxable income, you are eligible to contribute to an IRA. Taxable income includes wages, salaries, professional fees, commissions, taxable alimony, tips, and other income received from services. Taxable income does not include money from investments such as dividends, interest, rents, exchange of property, or retirement and annuity income.

Beginning with the 1998 tax year, you have the choice of three types of IRAs: to open or continue contributing to a traditional IRA; to start contributing to a new Roth IRA; or to contribute to both types of IRAs, as long as your annual contribution does not exceed $2,000.

TRADITIONAL IRA

The traditional IRA is a tax-deferred retirement account. You are eligible to establish and make contributions to a traditional IRA if you receive taxable income and you are under age 70 and 1/2. The contributions to your account can be deductible or nondeductible from your income, and the earnings accrue tax-deferred until distribution, when they are taxed as ordinary income.

Deductible contributions

Your contributions to a traditional IRA can be fully, partially, or not deductible from your pre-tax income. The total contributions can be as much as $4,000 a year for a married couple, even if one spouse has no income. The limit for each individual is $2,000.

You can contribute to a deductible IRA despite the fact that you or your spouse are covered by a qualified retirement plan during the year (assuming your income does not exceed the amount for a deductible IRA).

The table below (Table 3-1) shows the range of adjusted gross income (AGI) to make a fully deductible $2,000 IRA contribution.

TAX-DEDUCTIBLE IRA CONTRIBUTIONS

You can make a fully tax-deductible contribution to a traditional IRA if your AGI is equal to or less than:

Tax Year	Single Filers	Married Filing Jointly
1998	$30,000	$50,000
1999	$31,000	$51,000
2000	$32,000	$52,000
2001	$33,000	$53,000
2002	$34,000	$54,000
2003	$40,000	$60,000
2004	$45,000	$65,000
2005	$50,000	$70,000
2006	$50,000	$75,000
2007	$50,000	$80,000

Table 3-1

Nondeductible contributions

Nondeductible contributions to a traditional IRA do not lower your taxes, but they do allow you to take advantage of tax-deferred savings. The limit on nondeductible contributions is equal to your earned income or $2,000 ($4,000 for a spousal IRA), whichever is less, minus the amount of your deductible contribution. The advantage of a nondeductible IRA is that interest, dividends, and capital gains are tax-deferred until you withdraw them.

Withdrawals

If you have a traditional IRA, you can withdraw the assets in your account without penalty after age 59 and 1/2. Withdrawals before age 59 and 1/2 must be deposited in another qualified retirement plan or IRA within 60 days to avoid taxes and penalty.

Under certain conditions, however, you can make penalty free withdrawals from a traditional IRA before age 59 and 1/2. The conditions include the purchase of a home ($10,000 maximum withdrawl), qualified higher education, medical expenses, disability, or death.

Actually, you can begin withdrawals from a traditional IRA at any age without penalty if withdrawals are in equal amounts designed to exhaust your account during your lifetime. But early withdrawals probably won't produce much retirement income, especially if you've only contributed to your IRA a few years.

You must start withdrawing your money from a traditional IRA by April 1 following the year you are age 70 and 1/2 and stick to a minimum withdrawal schedule. When you begin withdrawals, the nondeductible portion of your IRA is not taxed, while the deductible portion is taxed as ordinary income.

ROTH IRA

The Roth IRA is probably the most sophisticated of all the tools available for retirement planning. In a traditional IRA, contributions may be deductible from taxable income, and earnings accumulate tax-deferred to be taxed as ordinary income upon their withdrawal. In contrast, contributions to a Roth IRA are not deductible but earnings accumulate tax free.

Additionally, unlike a traditional IRA, you can make contributions to a Roth IRA after age 70 and 1/2, and there is no requirement for minimum distributions at that age.

In fact, you can make annual contributions to both a traditional and a Roth IRA. However, the total contributions to both IRAs cannot exceed $2,000.

Income rules

Like the deductible, traditional IRA, there are income rules to open a Roth IRA. If you are a single tax filer earning under $95,000 per year, you can contribute a full $2,000 each year to a Roth IRA. This amount diminishes and gradually falls to zero for adjusted gross income ranging from $95,000 to $110,000. Similarly if you are married filing jointly, and the income of you and your spouse is less than $150,000, you can contribute $4,000 per year ($2,000 per IRA). The amount for married couple filing jointly phases out from $150,000 to $160,000.

Withdrawals

Since your contributions to a Roth IRA are from your after-tax income, you can withdraw these contributions at any time without paying taxes or a penalty. Moreover, you won't owe taxes or be penalized on the earnings you withdraw from a Roth IRA if your account has been established over five years and you are over age 59 and 1/2.

If your Roth IRA has been established at least 5 years, you can receive tax and penalty-free withdrawals before age 59 and 1/2 to apply toward the purchase of a first-time home (maximum withdrawl amount is $10,000), qualified higher education expenses, and in case of a death, or disability.

CHOOSING AN IRA

Deciding whether to contribute to a traditional or Roth IRA could be a tough decision. To begin with, you should consider a Roth IRA if you have a medium- to long-term investment horizon and at least five years until retirement. Also, a Roth Ira may be right for you if you don't qualify for a deductible, traditional IRA.

On the other hand, a deductible, traditional IRA might be your best choice if you want a long-term investment plan designed to provide maximum tax-deferred growth.

Deciding between a traditional and a Roth IRA also depends on your tax rate at retirement. A Roth IRA will generally provide more after-tax income than a traditional IRA if you are in a high tax bracket in retirement.

CONVERTING A TRADITIONAL IRA TO A ROTH IRA

You can convert all or part of a traditional IRA to a Roth IRA, but if your AGI is over $100,000 — whether you are married or single — the conversion option is not available. Before you decide to convert to a Roth IRA, here are some points to consider:

> * If you convert from a traditional to a Roth IRA, you must pay income taxes (but no early withdrawal penalty) on earnings and deductible contributions.

> * If you have only a short time until you retire and expect to draw on your IRA, it may not be wise to pay taxes on a Roth conversion.

> * If your Roth IRA is held for five years and you are past age 59 and 1/2, all withdrawals from the plan are tax free.

Chapter 4
BASICS OF RETIREMENT PLANS

Nothing beats a retirement free of financial worry. How is this possible? There are two requirements: The first requirement is to participate in the retirement plan where you work. The second one is to understand the basics of your retirement plan — how it works. The more you know about your plan, the more it could be worth when you retire.

If you have a defined-benefit plan, there is little you can do about your retirement income. In this type of plan, your employer sets aside money, usually based on your salary and years of service, for your retirement. In all probability, you'll have a defined-contribution retirement plan, and your employer may offer you a choice of investments, even matching a part or all of your contribution.

On the other hand, a defined-contribution plan provides more flexibility, tax savings, and a potentially greater retirement income than a defined-benefit plan. Regardless of your type of retirement plan, there are certain rules that apply.

BASIC RULES

Qualified Retirement Plans

Employers who sponsor qualified retirement plans and employees who participate in these plans receive special tax benefits. Employers can deduct all their contributions, within limits, from taxable income, and employees can defer paying income tax on their contributions. Employers and employees who participate in plans that are not qualified receive no special tax benefits.

To sponsor a qualified retirement plan, an employer must follow federal guidelines and provide the following minimum standards:

> * Be a permanent component of an employee's compensation program.

* Observe certain limitations on the payment of benefits.

* Provide vesting provisions for participants' contributions to the retirement plan.

* Assure that plan participants work a designated number of hours each year to qualify for benefits.

Eligibility requirements

Most employer-sponsored retirement plans require that you meet eligibility requirements before you participate. Usually, you can participate in a plan if you have one year of work with your employer, you work a required number of hours during the year, and you are age 21 or over.

Some education organizations may require an age of 26 and one year of work to participate in a retirement plan. Other education organizations may call for an age of 21 with three years of work. A year of work is generally defined as 1,000 hours of work during a 12-month period.

Employers do have the right to deny you participation in their retirement plan. However, exclusion may only be for conditions that do not constitute discrimination.

Retirement plan managers

Who administers your retirement plan? First is the sponsor of the plan, your employer. Your employer may be a company, school, small business, nonprofit organization, or the government.

Second, a plan administrator, designated by your employer, handles your contributions, makes distributions, and ensures the plan complies with federal and state regulations.

The plan administrator may use an independent firm such as a bank, mutual fund, or insurance company, to handle all or part of your retirement money.

Finally, there is the retirement benefits representative where you work. This person is your main contact for information about your plan.

Summary plan description

If you participate in a retirement plan, you are entitled by law to receive a summary plan description (a booklet) that contains information on your plan. It describes how the plan works, when you are eligible to retire, how to calculate your retirement benefits, and how to file for benefits. You'll also receive periodic updates of the booklet that reflect changes in your retirement plan.

Benefit's statement

You will receive a benefit's statement each year that shows the assets in your retirement plan and whether you have a permanent right to receive them. If you want to receive a statement more often than yearly, you must request it in writing to your plan administrator.

Payroll deductions

The most convenient way to fund your retirement plan is through payroll deduction. In this arrangement, your employer sets aside a percentage of your income for your retirement. The percentage may come from your salary or from bonuses or commissions. To set up a payroll deduction plan, check with your retirement benefits representative.

Vesting

Vesting is your nonforfeitable right to the benefits that you accrue in an employer-sponsored retirement plan. You usually have to work several years to become fully vested. Each year that you work, you accrue more benefit credits and become more vested in your company's retirement plan.

Vesting schedule

The contributions that your employer makes to your retirement must be vested according to schedules that are required by law for both defined-benefit and defined-contribution retirement plans. It usually takes five to seven years, depending on your employer's vesting schedule, before you are fully vested.

There are two vesting schedules. The first schedule, cliff vesting, requires that you be fully vested in five years. The second, graded vesting, requires full vesting in seven years.

If your retirement plan requires seven years of employment to be fully vested, for example, you may be 40 percent vested at the end of four years. At the end of six years 80 percent, with full vestment of 100 percent after seven years of employment. When you are fully vested, the benefits that your employer contributes to your retirement are legally yours. Any contributions you make to your retirement plan are, of course, always fully vested. Although full vesting must occur after seven years, you cannot receive full retirement benefits until you actually retire.

ROLLOVERS

Tax-free rollover

A tax-free rollover will safeguard your retirement assets from an early withdrawal penalty and 20 percent federal withholding tax. You can use a tax-free rollover to move your retirement savings from one qualified retirement plan to another qualified retirement plan; a qualified plan to an IRA; an IRA to a qualified plan; or an IRA to an IRA.

IRA rollover

An IRA rollover is the easiest way to avoid an early withdrawal penalty and a withholding tax. This involves moving your money from a qualified retirement plan to an IRA. You can use an IRA rollover for these reasons:

* Retirement.

* Company layoff.

* Your company is terminating its retirement plan.

* A job change.

* You have become disabled.

Job Changes And Retirement Benefits

Like many employees, you may change jobs a few times during your career. Although you may be fully vested when you leave your job, the age when you receive your retirement benefits depends on whether your plan has an immediate or deferred payout (the method your employer chooses to distribute your retirement benefits).

An immediate payout allows you to receive your retirement benefits immediately, regardless of your age. With a deferred payout, your benefits are frozen until you reach retirement age. In this case, your benefits will be eroded by inflation when you actually start receiving them.

If you change jobs, you'll have to decide whether to transfer your retirement assets to your new employer, leave them with your last employer if possible, or rollover your assets to an IRA.

Break In Service

Any interruption in your employment or failure to work a required number of hours could result in a loss of your retirement benefits. To protect employees, the Employment Retirement Income Security Act (ERISA) has rules governing what constitutes a "break in service." As a rule, a "break in service" is usually defined as a 12-month period in which the participant in a retirement plan worked less than 500 hours. The 12-month period can be a calendar year or other consecutive 12-month period designated by the plan.

Early Retirement

There are two ways to retire early: when your company allows you to end your employment before normal retirement age which is usually 65 and when your company reduces its workforce. Thus, you may be eligible for early retirement at age 60 with 10 years of employment while normal retirement age might be 65 with 10 years of employment.

Early retirement benefits

ERISA does not require retirement plans to provide early retirement benefits. Therefore, plans that do offer early retirement are generally free to establish their own eligibility rules for the payment of benefits. However, ERISA does require that early retirement benefits must be at least the actuarial equivalent of normal retirement benefits. That is, the plan must first compute the monthly benefits expected to be payable at normal retirement age and then reduce that amount for such factors as an employee's age and years of service.

Defined-benefit reduction

If you have a defined-benefit plan and retire before normal retirement age, you will have a reduction in your benefits. The reduction is usually based on a percentage times the number of years left until you are eligible for normal retirement. Your income might be reduced as much as 20 percent if you retire at age 60 instead of 65. This could be calculated by multiplying the number of years (5) that you retired early (before 65) by four percent, the figure that your company might set for early retirement. In a typical retirement plan, your retirement income could almost double between ages 60 and 65.

BENEFICIARY OPTIONS

Retirement plans that provide benefits in the form of an annuity must provide beneficiary options. This means if you are partially or fully vested, your spouse will automatically receive survivor benefits if you die unless you and your spouse have declined the survivor option in writing. Here are some additional beneficiary options that apply to annuities:

> * If you have been married for at least one year, federal law requires that death benefits from your retirement plan be paid to your spouse. With the consent of your spouse, you can name someone other than your spouse as your beneficiary.

> * If you are married and want death benefits paid to someone other than your spouse or in addition to your spouse, your spouse must agree to this in writing.

> * If you are not married, you have the option to name one or more beneficiaries. Should you then become married, the beneficiary designations are void one year after your marriage.

RETIREMENT BENEFITS

Defined-benefit plans

A defined-benefit retirement plan may allow you to retire as early as 55 to 60, or require you to work until age 65. The retirement income paid by a defined-benefit plan is usually calculated by a formula that considers your earnings, years of work, and age at retirement.

If you receive Social Security, some defined-benefit plans will reduce your retirement income by the amount of the payment. However, your retirement income is usually not decreased because of an increase in your Social Security payment.

The most generous defined-benefit plans are those based on your salary during your highest paid three to five working years. The least generous are those based on your average salary over your entire career.

A "fair" benefit should provide you retirement income equal to one percent of your average salary during your three to five highest paid years times the number of years you worked. For example, if you worked 30 years and your average salary for the highest paid five years was $50,000, your retirement income would be $15,000.

Defined-contribution plans

If you have a defined-contribution plan, the amount of your retirement benefits will depend on how much you contribute to the plan, and how well you invest your money. A defined-contribution plan may give you the choice of receiving your benefits in an annuity or a lump sum.

If you receive your retirement benefits in an annuity, the minimum amount of your distributions is determined by your account balance at the beginning of the year divided by your life expectancy or the joint life expectancy of you and your beneficiary. Life expectancy tables are found in IRS Publication 575, Pensions and Annuity Income.

If you have more than one defined-contribution plan, you'll have to combine the plans to arrive at a total figure for tax purposes. You can simplify the paperwork by a trustee-to-trustee transfer or IRA rollover to combine all your accounts under one IRA. When you don't combine your accounts, you'll have to add up their individual values to determine the amount of your monthly distributions.

Annuity options

If you receive your retirement benefits as an annuity, there are usually three payment options. The first and most popular option is life only which pays a specified amount until your death. The second option is joint and survivor which reduces your benefits but provides benefits to your spouse should you die first. Finally, there is a life and certain period option that pays annuity benefits for your lifetime or for a fixed number of years, whichever comes first.

Inflation adjustments

The distributions from most retirement plans are not adjusted for inflation. A few plans, such as those of the federal government, are adjusted yearly for inflation. Periodic raises for inflation are an important factor to consider if you transfer your retirement benefits from one employer to another.

Prohibited benefit reductions

ERISA prohibits retirement plan amendments that could cause a reduction in the benefits you accrue. As a rule, a plan amendment that reduces benefits you accrue before adoption of the amendment is prohibited if the amendment eliminates an optional form of benefit. For example, an optional form of benefit could be a lump-sum distribution, or the amendment eliminates or reduces an early retirement benefit or a retirement-type subsidy.

LUMP-SUM DISTRIBUTIONS

Whether you are retiring or going to a new job, you may have a choice of receiving you retirement benefits as an annuity or in a lump sum. A lump-sum distribution is the distribution in one year of the total assets in your retirement plan.

If you have a defined-benefit retirement plan, your employer may require that you receive your benefits as an annuity in equal monthly payments. You are more likely to have the choice of a lump-sum distribution if you have a defined-contribution plan.

If you have a choice, should you receive your retirement benefits as an annuity or lump sum? A lump-sum distribution has an advantage over an annuity because you can rollover a lump-sum into an IRA. That way you can withdraw the money as you need it and the balance will continue to earn tax-deferred interest. Also, you may be eligible for favorable five or ten year income averaging if you receive a lump-sum distribution.

INCOME AVERAGING

If your retirement benefits are paid in a lump sum, it's important to know whether you will receive them in the calendar year you retire or spread over more than one year. If you receive a lump sum over more than one year, you may not be eligible for favorable five or ten year income averaging. With income averaging, a lump sum is taxed as if you receive it over a period of years rather than all at once.

DISTRIBUTIONS AND TAXES

The distributions from your retirement plan are fully taxable after you recover any contributions you made to the plan. If you made no contributions to your plan, all of your distributions are taxable.

The retirement plans which are partly taxed are those where both you and your employer made contributions. If you receive a partly taxable distribution, your employer usually computes the taxable portion and reports it to you.

GOVERNMENT OVERSIGHT

Employee Retirement Income Security Act (ERISA)

In 1974, Congress passed ERISA to protect the interests of participants (and their beneficiaries) in retirement plans. The Act is administered by the U.S. Department of Labor, the Internal Revenue Service, and a nonprofit government organization, the Pension Benefit Guaranty Corporation. The purpose of ERISA is to provide rights and guarantee retirement benefits to workers. Some of the more important

ERISA rules include the following:

* The age and service requirements for participants in a retirement plan should be reasonable and documented by provisions.

* Those employees who work for a specified minimum period under a retirement plan will receive some benefits at retirement. Their benefits could include vesting, benefit accrual, and break in service provisions.

* Money will be available to pay retirement benefits.

* Retirement plan funds should be handled prudently through fiduciary (trustee) provisions.

* Employees who participate in a retirement plan can exercise their rights without harassment or interference.

* Plan participants and their beneficiaries must be informed of their rights and entitlements under their plans.

* Spouses of retirees are protected through joint and survivor provisions.

* Participants in a retirement plan can appeal if denied benefits.

* Plan participants can sue in federal court to recover benefits.

Source: U.S. Department of Labor

Pension Benefit Guaranty Corporation (PBGC)

The PBGC was created under ERISA to provide insurance protection to participants in a retirement plan. PBGC insures the vested   benefits of employees and retirees in certain defined-benefit retirement plans. If a plan covered by the PBGC terminates or lacks the money to pay vested retirement benefits, the PBGC will guarantee benefit payments up to a statutory limit.

In addition, a plan participant is protected by the PBGC when a merger, consolidation, or transfer of assets or liabilities from one retirement plan to another occurs. In this situation, the accrued benefits of the participant cannot be lower than the benefits prior to the merger, consolidation, or transfer of assets or liabilities.

You can receive additional information about your retirement rights and benefits by contacting:

Pension and Welfare Benefits Administration
Division of Technical Assistance and Inquiries
Room N-5625
U.S. Department of Lab
200 Constitution Avenue, N.W.,
Washington, D.C. 20210

Chapter 5

INVESTMENT CHOICES

Which investments should you choose for your retirement plan? Should you invest in a money market fund, a stock, or a bond fund? In most cases, it depends on your type of retirement plan.

If you have a defined-benefit retirement plan, you probably won't have a choice of investments. That's because a defined-benefit plan is usually funded entirely by the employer.

It's more likely that you'll have a defined-contribution plan and your employer will offer you several investment choices for your retirement dollars. The following are the usual kinds of investments offered in defined-contribution plans.

GUARANTEED INVESTMENT CONTRACTS

Guaranteed Investment Contracts (GICs), sometimes named "guaranteed interest accounts," are an investment choice in most defined-contribution retirement plans. In this type of investment, you buy a GIC from an insurance company. In turn, the insurance company guarantees the interest rate on your GIC for a certain period, usually from one to seven years.

The insurance company invests your GIC money in government bonds, corporate bonds, mortgages, and sometimes lower grade bonds. They then receive part of the income from your GIC investment and deliver the rest to your retirement account.

You should keep in mind that the money you invest in a GIC isn't guaranteed - only the interest that your money earns is guaranteed.

GIC interest rates

The interest rate for each GIC deposit is the rate in effect on the date your money is received by the insurance company. So each deposit you make during the year could have a different interest rate.

After you make your last GIC deposit during the year, the insurance company will determine your composite interest rate. This is a single rate based on the amount, timing, and interest paid on each of your deposits and the guaranteed rate for all the money in your account. The composite rate continues to the end of the guaranteed period.

The following is an example of how a GIC works (Table 5-1). Let's assume that you have a five year GIC, your deposit year is from January 1 to December 31, and you make four $100 deposits to your account at varying interest rates.

Date	Deposit Amount	Interest Rate	Interest Earned by December 31
January 1	$100	5.00%	$5.00
April 1	$100	6.00%	$4.50
July 1	$100	4.50%	$2.50
October 1	$100	5.50%	$1.50

Composite interest rate = 3.37 percent

Table 5-1

In the example of how a GIC works, the composite interest rate on your investment is 3.37 percent. This is the guaranteed rate for the next four years. A new GIC account begins at the start of each new deposit year and works the same way. Thus, you could have many GICs after several years, each with its own interest rate. As each account matures at the end of its guaranteed period, you could then put the money into a new GIC account or move it to another type of investment.

Withdrawals from GICs

If you withdraw money from your GIC account before the end of the guaranteed period, you could be subject to a surrender charge. This charge is assessed only if the interest rate for a new GIC deposit is higher than your account's guaranteed rate.

Disadvantages of GICs

It's easy to see that GICs have their disadvantages. First, if your money is invested in a low yielding GIC that extends for several years, interest rates could move higher. This means that the money you invest in a GIC could be earning about 3.5 percent when the interest rate on other investments is six or seven percent. In effect, you are losing 2.5 to 3.5 percent on your GIC investment.

A second drawback to GICs is their risk. GICs are only as safe as the insurance company that issues them, and some companies have been burdened with financial problems. So there is always the possibility that you will outlive the insurance company.

A final disadvantage involves inflation. With the shrinking value of the dollar, a GIC pays a small rate of return. That's because your after tax return on a GIC will barely outpace rising prices.

GICs may have a place in your retirement account if you invest in them when interest rates are relatively high, you don't withdraw your money before the end of the guaranteed period, and the insurance company that issues the GIC is financially sound.

CERTIFICATES OF DEPOSIT

Certificates of Deposit (CDs) are like GICs because they pay interest for a pre-determined period at a specified rate. While GICs are not federally insured, CDs are insured up to $100,000.

The problem with CDs is the same as with GICs: your money is invested for several months or even years at a set rate. Thus, if you invest in a long-term CD and interest rates rise, the return on the CD would be less than many other investments.

TAX-DEFERRED ANNUITIES

Tax-deferred annuities which are usually issued by insurance companies consist of two types: fixed, with a set interest rate like a CD; and variable, which pays interest at an unspecified rate. Variable annuities are the ones frequently offered by retirement plans. Both types are tax-deferred.

Fixed annuities

With a fixed annuity, your money receives an interest rate that's guaranteed for an initial period, usually one to three years. When the period ends, the insurance company determines a new interest rate for the next period. Unlike variable annuities, the assets of fixed annuities are invested in the insurance company's general account and are subject to creditor's claims.

Variable annuities

Variable annuities allow you a choice of investments. Usually, you have the option to invest in stock, bond, and money market mutual funds. In addition, a variable annuity will allow you to switch among the investment choices tax free. Since variable annuities generally invest in mutual funds, their value will increase or decrease as the funds change in price.

Annuity benefits

In retirement, your annuity benefits should continue for several years, depending on the value of your account and the amount of your withdrawals. The benefits are fixed and guaranteed by the assets of the insurance company that holds the annuity.

Whether you receive an annuity in a lump sum, monthly, or at other intervals, your after-tax contributions are tax free and the rest of your benefits are taxable.

Advantages of annuities

One advantage to an annuity is that any interest, dividends, and capital gains paid to your account are tax-deferred. Another is that an annuity is issued by an insurance company so your assets are passed to your estate or beneficiary as if they were insurance.

Disadvantages of annuities

Some of the disadvantages of an annuity include the following:

* Since the assets of insurance companies are not insured, there is always the chance you could lose all or part of your investment in an annuity.

* Except for immediate and heavy financial hardships, you are generally subject to a 10 percent penalty tax should you withdraw money from an annuity before age 59 and 1/2.

* Some insurance companies have a penalty for withdrawals during the first few years after you start an annuity.

* Annuities generally have high management fees.

* Annuities seldom provide a cost-of-living adjustment.

MUTUAL FUNDS

A mutual fund is an investment company that pools money from shareholders to invest mainly in securities offered by corporations. The number of securities in a fund may range from as few as 25 to 50 up to a few hundred. When you buy shares in a mutual fund, you own a portion of the securities held in the fund. As the securities in the fund move up and down in price, the value of the fund changes accordingly. Most retirement plans offer various kinds of mutual funds. These usually include: growth, balanced, growth and income funds; corporate bond, zero-coupon bond funds; and money market funds.

Growth funds

Growth funds are the most popular type of mutual fund. They invest primarily in the common stock of companies whose sales and earnings are growing rapidly. These funds seek maximum capital gains through an increase in the value of the stocks held in the fund.

The main objective of growth funds is capital appreciation, not current income. They are a medium risk investment, and many growth funds have good long-term performance records.

Balanced funds

Balanced funds usually have three investment objectives: to conserve your initial investment, pay income, and seek long-term growth of both principal and income. To achieve those objectives, balanced funds invest in a combination of common stocks, preferred stocks, and bonds. They are for the conservative income-oriented retirement account.

Growth and income funds

Growth and income funds invest in well-established companies and those that have a good record of paying high dividends. These funds avoid investing in stocks that pay no dividends, trying to strike a balance between achieving capital gains and dividend income. The per share value of growth and income funds may show less increase than growth funds, but they usually provide more income than growth funds.

Corporate bond funds

A corporate bond fund pools money from shareholders to invest primarily in the bonds of corporations. These funds usually provide relatively high returns and maintain moderately stable values. However, the value of a corporate bond fund may decrease when interest rates rise and increase when interest rates drop. So over short periods, price changes can be large if interest rates rise or fall rapidly. Yet, over the long-term, these price changes tend to even out.

Before you invest in a corporate bond fund, it's a good idea to check the quality of the bonds. You can do this by calling a bond rating company such as Standard and Poor's at (212) 208-1527 or Moody's at (212) 553-0300. Any bond rated lower than BBB by Standard and Poor's or Baa by Moody's is considered investment grade (see page 71).

If you invest in a fund that holds investment grade bonds, not only do you have a high degree of assurance that you'll not lose money, but the fund's return will be greater than many other investments. Therefore, a corporate bond fund could be a good investment to have in your retirement account.

Zero-coupon bond funds

A zero-coupon bond fund invests in debt securities issued at a discount from their face value. For example, a fund might pay $100 for a $1,000 zero-coupon bond that yields 12 percent and matures in 20 years.

The interest on a zero-coupon bond fund is compounded and paid in a lump sum when the bonds held in the fund mature. Like corporate bonds, zero-coupons are rated by Standard and Poor's and Moody's on their worth or ability to pay interest.

As with other mutual funds, you can sell your zero-coupon shares anytime, and transfer the proceeds to another type of investment in your retirement plan. Or you can decide to hold your shares in the fund to maturity, when you will receive the full face value.

Since zero-coupon bond funds pay a relatively high rate of interest, you could consider them for your retirement account. This assumes, of course, that the bonds in the fund are investment grade.

Money market mutual funds

Money market mutual funds invest in bank CDs, commercial paper (short-term IOUs) issued by large corporations, treasury bills and notes, and bankers' acceptances (used to finance international commercial transactions).

Since the price per share of a money market fund is held constant at $1 you cannot receive less than your original investment. In contrast, the price of a stock or bond fund rises and falls as the securities held in these funds change in value and you could receive less than what you invested.

There are three reasons why money market funds are good investments for your retirement account: they provide a "fair" return; they can serve as a temporary investment while you are deciding where to invest permanently for retirement and; they can serve as a reserve fund to add money to a stock or bond fund when its price is relatively low.

Although money market funds are a safe and stable investment, their long-term return is usually less than that of a stock or bond fund. Therefore, it's wise to limit your investment in a money market fund to not over 25 percent of your retirement account.

It's easy to see why mutual funds are widely held in retirement accounts. They are professionally managed and their risk is reduced because they hold a variety of securities. They are liquid (easily converted to cash) and their price is listed daily in most large newspapers. They offer the greatest return of all the investment choices for a defined-contribution retirement plan.

Part Two
SUPPLEMENTING YOUR
RETIREMENT INCOME

You can never be too
rich or too thin.

–Duchess of Windsor

Chapter 6

MUTUAL FUNDS
THE IDEAL RETIREMENT SUPPLEMENT

If you are like many people, the income from your pension plan and Social Security won't be enough to cover all your expenses in retirement. The chances are you'll need personal investments to supplement your retirement income.

Investing in mutual funds is one of the best ways to supplement your retirement income. There are two general types of mutual funds: closed-end and open-end. Closed-end funds have a fixed number of shares and usually trade on a stock exchange. Open-end funds, the more popular of the two types, have an unlimited number of shares and are not listed on an exchange. This book covers only open-end funds since they usually provide a greater return than closed-end funds.

TYPES OF OPEN-END FUNDS

Since there are so many open-end mutual funds, it's difficult to classify all of them by type or their investment objective. A fund with an objective to invest in small growth companies, for example, also may hold stocks of medium-sized growth companies. Another fund could have an objective to provide its shareholders with maximum dividend income but invest in companies that pay relatively low dividends. Here is a list of the more common types of funds and their investment objective:

> Aggressive growth fund — maximum capital gains, current income is not a primary factor.

> Balanced funds — current income and long-term capital gains.

> Corporate bond funds — a high level of income from corporate and government bonds.

GNMA or Ginnie Mae Funds — income from mortgage securities backed by the Government National Mortgage Association (GNMA).

Global equity funds — income from securities traded worldwide, including the U.S.

Growth funds — long-term capital appreciation from investments mainly in common stocks.

Growth and income funds — a combination of capital appreciation with steady income.

Income (stock) funds — income from dividend paying stocks.

Index funds — capital appreciation and income by matching the performance of a stock market index, such as the Standard & Poor's 500 Index.

Money market mutual funds — current income, liquidity, and safety.

Small company funds — asset growth through investing in companies with low market capitalization.

You can request a copy of *The Directory of Mutual Funds* from the Investment Company Institute 1401 H Street, N.W., Washington, D.C. 20005, telephone number 202-326-5800. This publication, which costs $10.00, contains helpful information about investing in mutual funds.

REGULATION OF MUTUAL FUNDS

Federal and state laws regulate the activities of mutual funds. These laws require the disclosure of fund operations to the Securities and Exchange Commission (SEC), state regulators, and fund shareholders. There are four federal laws that regulate mutual funds:

* Securities Act of 1933 requires that all mutual funds file a registration statement and provide information to the SEC. It also requires that funds provide current and potential investors with a prospectus that describes the fund's management, investment objectives, and policy.

* Securities Exchange Act of 1934 makes funds liable for anti-fraud provisions and regulations by the SEC and the National Association of Securities Dealers.

* Investment Advisors Act of 1940 regulates the actions of mutual fund investment advisors.

* Investment Company Act of 1940 prevents conflicts of interest and self-dealing in the management of mutual funds.

MUTUAL FUND PROSPECTUS

A mutual fund cannot sell you shares until it first sends you a prospectus, the official document that describes a fund and its policies. A prospectus should provide enough information for you to decide if you want to invest in the fund. It's a good idea to check more than one prospectus so you will select the fund that meets your investment objective.

ADVANTAGES OF MUTUAL FUNDS

Professional Management

A board of directors is responsible for administering a fund's investment policy and selecting the fund's manager. The manager is a full-time and experienced professional who follows a disciplined investment strategy.

Fund managers usually have access to the latest information about securities and base their investment decisions on factors such as the growth potential of particular industries, earnings outlook for individual securities, and general economic conditions.

There are few individual investors who can compete with the experience and skill of fund managers.

Diversification

Diversification is an investment principle that requires holding more than one type of security to reduce risk. Mutual fund managers diversify their portfolios by investing in a variety of stocks, bonds, and cash equivalents. When you own shares in a fund, you automatically own a portion of several securities, a diversified investment.

Convenience

It's easy to invest in a fund. You can handle the paperwork to open an account and make later investments from your home. The fund takes care of the bookkeeping and provides you a statement after each investment as well as yearly reports.

To open an account, telephone or write a fund and ask for a free prospectus. If the prospectus meets your investment objectives, complete the application and return it to the fund.

Low Initial Investment

Most funds have a minimum initial investment for regular accounts. A few funds have no minimum, and others require as much as several hundred dollars. However, most funds set their minimum between $500 and $1,000. The minimum for most IRAs is usually less than for a regular account, about $250. Later investments are much lower than the minimum, usually from $50 to $100.

Automatic Monthly Investments

An easy way to invest in mutual funds is to ask your bank or employer to make regular payments to your fund. Most banks will honor the automatic transfer of money from your checking account. Also, your employer may have a payroll deduction plan that will automatically deduct money from your salary and send it to your fund.

Automatic Reinvestment of Distributions

If you choose, you can reinvest all or part of the dividend and capital gain distributions paid by your fund to buy additional shares. Distributions are reinvested with the use of a fund's dividend reinvestment plan (DRIP). A DRIP is a good strategy because it gives you the opportunity not only to acquire more shares but also prevents you from spending the distributions if you receive them in cash. There is no minimum investment requirement when you reinvest distributions.

Conversion Privileges

Many funds are part of a family of funds. The family may consist of stock, bond, global, specialty, commodities, and money market funds. If your fund belongs to a family, you usually can exchange one fund for another within the family. Since your retirement goals may change through the years, a conversion privilege is an important feature.

Liquidity

You can cash in all or part of your fund's shares at any time. The value you receive will be the current market value of your shares, which could be more or less than what you invested. Most funds will redeem shares upon a written request. However, when the redemption exceeds a specific amount, many funds require a signature guarantee.

Automatic Withdrawal Plans

Many funds have a withdrawal plan that allows you to receive payments at regular intervals. You can receive payments from dividends, capital gains, or sell shares of your fund on a monthly or quarterly basis. An automatic withdrawal plan is a convenient way to add to your retirement income.

Recordkeeping

Mutual funds keep good records for their shareholders. You will receive a confirmation from the fund when you make an investment, redeem shares, or exchange one fund for another. Depending on the fund's policy, you will also receive an update of your account on a quarterly, semi-annual, or yearly basis.

SELECTING A FUND

When you choose a mutual fund, there are several items you should consider. The first one is to select a fund that is compatible with your risk level.

Match your objective with your risk level

There is no magic formula for selecting the mutual fund that's right for you. However, you'll find it's not difficult if you first determine your investment objective and then the amount of risk you feel comfortable with.

Your objective should match that of the fund you select. A fund's prospectus contains a section titled "objectives" that explains how the fund intends to make money. If your objective is to accumulate $25,000 within fifteen years, consider a growth fund.

On the other hand, if you are about ready to retire and need extra income, a growth and income fund may be better.

Once you decide on your objective, determine your level of risk. If you worry a lot about your investments, then you probably have a low risk level. In this case, a growth and income fund may be better. Should you want even greater safety and more income, select an income fund. If you are the type of investor who can handle the price fluctuations of the more volatile funds, you probably have a high risk level. In this situation, consider a growth fund.

Performance

The most important selection criteria is a fund's past performance -its track record. Although the past performance of a fund doesn't always indicate future results, it is still the best measure to use when you select a fund. It's better to consider only those funds that have been good performers for several years. You'll find that some funds perform well for a year or two, but their overall performance is poor. The SEC requires funds to report their performance using a standard format. This makes it easier for you to compare the return on those funds that meet your investment objective.

When you compare funds, look at their total return which includes the reinvestment of dividend and capital gain distributions. The total return is expressed as a percentage for certain periods, usually quarterly and yearly.

You'll find that a fund's total return is measured against a market index such as the Standard and Poor's (S&P) 500, an industry norm for measuring average stock market performance. It's probably wise to invest only in those funds that have consistently provided a better return than the S&P 500.

Cost

There are two types of open-end funds: load and no-load. As the name suggests, load funds charge a commission (front-end load) when you purchase shares. They are usually sold by full-service brokers, insurance agents, or financial advisers. You can avoid paying a commission if you invest in no-load funds. With no-load funds, you deal directly with the funds so you don't pay a commission.

In addition to commissions there are other fees that some funds assess. If you want to reduce your investment expenses, it's a good idea to become familiar with the following fees:

–Management and customer service fee. This is a fee that you pay the investment company for the management and services that a fund provides. Since both load and no-load funds have this fee, it cannot be avoided. In the prospectus, the fee is listed as a percentage of the fund's net assets and totals about 0.75 to 1.75 percent.

–Front-end load. This is a sales charge or commission ranging from 1 percent to 8.5 percent that a fund deducts from each investment. For example, if your initial investment is $1,000 and the commission is 5 percent, your actual investment is only $950. What's more, the fund levies the commission on later investments and the reinvestment of distributions. Over the years, commissions can amount to a lot of money, money that is deducted from your investments with no benefit to you.

–Back-end load. This is a fee that some funds assess when shares are redeemed. It can range from 4 percent to 6.5 percent of the value of the redemption. Funds that don't have front-end loads often assess back-end loads to hide their commissions.

12b-1 fee. This fee is also known as a hidden load. The original intent of the fee was to aid funds with their marketing and distribution expenses. Whatever its original intent, many funds use the fee to extract additional money from the unwary investor. A 12b-1 fee can total as much as 1 percent of your investment.

Usually a fund does not charge a high front-end load in addition to the maximum allowable 12b-1 fee. Instead, a 12b-1 fee is combined with a back-end load as an alternative to a large front-end load. Let's see how fees can affect the amount you invest in a load fund. We'll take a hypothetical situation and assume you make a lump-sum investment of $1,000 in a 5 percent load fund that has a redemption fee of 5 percent, 12b-1 fee of 1 percent, and service charge of 1 percent. Let's further assume that you sell the fund after you've held it one year with no change in its price.

* Front-end load on initial investment (5 percent of $1,000) $50
* Back-end load (5 percent of $915) $46
* 12b-1 fee (1 percent of $1,000) $10
* Management and customer service fee (1 percent) $10
* Total charges $116
* Amount you receive at redemption $884
* Percent of loss on your $1,000 investment   11.6%

An investment of $1,000 in your hypothetic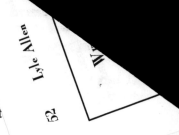
pare these charges to a pure no-load fund — a fu.
fee, or back-end load. The pure no-load fund asses.
vice fee of $10.

When you invest in a fund, there is no valid reaso.
1 fee, or back-end load. Read a fund's prospectus carefu
than a management and customer service charge, reject

Services

Another item to consider when you select a fund is th   ervices that
the fund offers its shareholders. You'll find that most no-loa .unds provide convenient and reliable services. Also, there is no high-pressure sales tactics by their
representatives.

You can handle most of the services that no-load funds provide by mail or telephone. You can open an account with a fund and make investments by mail. You can
usually sell all or part of your shares in a fund by telephone. You can switch from
one fund to another by telephone. Before you open an account, make certain the fund
provides all of the services that you want.

PURE NO-LOAD FUNDS

The two lists that follow include many pure no-load funds — funds that have no
front-end load, 12b-1 fee, or back-end load. The first list contains growth funds and

SELECTED GROWTH AND INCOME FUNDS
WITH NO FRONT-END LOAD, 12B-1 FEE, OR BACK-END LOAD

FUND	FIVE-YEAR ANNUALIZED TOTAL RETURN*	800 TELEPHONE NUMBER
AARP Growth & Income	17.8	322-2282
Fidelity Growth & Income	22.4	544-8888
Harbor Value	17.6	422-1050
Neuberger & Berman Guardian	13.5	877-9700
Safeco Equity	21.6	426-6730
Schwab 1000	22.4	435-4000
Scudder Growth & Income	17.6	225-2470
SteinRoe Growth & Income	18.8	338-2550
Strong Total Return	18.6	368-1030
T. Rowe Price Growth & Income	17.1	638-5660
Vanguard Windsor II	21.0	851-4999

* Note: includes change in net asset value and reinvestment of distributions for the period
ending December 31, 1998.

Table 6-1

SELECTED GROWTH FUNDS
TH NO FRONT-END LOAD, 12-B-1 FEE, OR BACK-END LOAD

FUND	FIVE-YEAR ANNUALIZED TOTAL RETURN *	800 TELEPHONE NUMBER
AARP Capital Growth	18.8	322-2282
American Century-20th Growth	18.9	345-2021
American Century-20th Select	19.2	345-2021
Babson Growth	21.2	422-2766
Columbia Growth	21.0	547-1707
Fairmont	9.9	262-9936
Fidelity Disciplined Equity	19.8	544-8888
Janus Mercury	26.4	525-8983
Janus Twenty	29.6	525-8983
Montgomery Growth	17.4	575-3863
Safeco Growth Fund	18.5	426-6730
Scudder Large Company Growth	21.9	225-2470
SteinRoe Growth Stock	21.1	338-2550
Strong Opportunity	16.9	368-1030
T. Rowe Price New America	17.3	638-5660
Vanguard-U.S. Growth	25.8	851-4999

* Note: includes change in net asset value and reinvestment of distributions for the period ending December 31, 1998.

Table 6-2

the second one growth and income funds. The lists provide a good starting point for the selection of a fund. You can get a free prospectus by calling the telephone number listed in tables 6-1 and 6-2.

FAMILY OF FUNDS

Many mutual funds are part of a larger grouping named a "family" of funds. All funds within the family have a different portfolio manager but are under the direction of the same investment company. A family could include growth stock, corporate bond, global, and money market funds.

When you invest in a fund that belongs to a family, usually you can switch from one fund to another within the family. The opportunity to switch funds is valuable because your investment goals may change through the years. Also, most families maintain a money market fund that you can use as an emergency fund or cash reserve.

Here's a list of pure no-load fund families that sponsor growth, growth and income, and money market funds. You can receive a prospectus on any of these funds by calling the number listed in the table.

SELECTED NO-LOAD FUND FAMILIES WITH GROWTH AND MONEY MARKET FUNDS

FUND FAMILY	800 TELEPHONE NUMBER
American Century-20th Century	345-2021
Columbia	547-1707
Fidelity	544-8888
Janus	525-8983
Neuberger & Berman	877-9700
T. Rowe Price	638-5660
Scudder	225-2470
SteinRoe	338-2550
Strong	368-1030
Vanguard	851-4999

Table 6-3

SOURCES OF INFORMATION

Where can you find more information on mutual funds? The place to start is with the fund itself. Since a fund's prospectus contains its annual return according to a standard format, it's easy to compare the performance of different funds. How do you get a prospectus? You call the fund and ask for one. Also, many libraries have information on funds, including their address and telephone number.

In addition, there are several publications that cover funds. Here are some of them.

* *Standard and Poor's Stock Guide* provides statistical information on about 700 funds. This guide, issued monthly, classifies funds by their investment objective, total assets, high/low price per share for the last five years, minimum investment required, sales fees, the return on an assumed investment of $10,000 for the past five years, and much more.

* *Investor's Business Daily* devotes a section to funds. In each issue, the newspaper includes the performance rankings of funds, current price per share, percent of price change during the year, type of fund, and a mutual fund index that tracks the performance of several types of funds.

* *Forbes* and *Business Week* publish a yearly ranking of funds according to their performance, risk, and other factors.

* Other sources for information on funds include *Morningstar's Barron's, Mutual Fund Values, Weisenberger's Investment Companies, and United Mutual Fund Selector.*

Chapter 7

DOLLAR-COST AVERAGING PLUS
AN INVESTMENT STRATEGY
FOR A WEALTHY RETIREMENT

There are various ways to retire wealthy, but one of the best is investing in mutual funds. Building wealth in funds is not a result of a one-time investment, nor is it achieved instantly. Rather, it is primarily the outcome of investing regularly, for the long term, according to an investment strategy.

Dollar-Cost Averaging Plus (DCAP) is a new strategy for investing in mutual funds. DCAP is not a "get rich quick scheme," but a formula for long-term investing in funds. It functions on the belief that the trend of most mutual fund prices is up, that within this trend, funds will experience up and down price volatility. Because of this volatility, the DCAP formula requires that you increase the amount of your investments when prices are relatively low and level-off investments when prices are high.

One feature of the DCAP formula is that it relieves you of trying to decide the right time to invest in a mutual fund. You can invest in a fund at any time when you use the formula.

Although the formula is an investment strategy that works best with mutual funds, you also can use it to buy individual shares of stock. Whether you use the formula to buy shares in funds or stocks, it could help you become wealthy.

DCAP FORMULA VS TYPICAL DOLLAR-COST AVERAGING

There are many methods you can use to invest in mutual funds. Typical dollar-cost averaging and lump-sum payment are two of the more popular ones. There are always ways to improve these methods, and that is what makes the DCAP formula so effective. DCAP is a refinement on the typical and often used method of dollar-cost averaging.

The typical method of dollar-cost averaging has been in use for many years and is a common way to invest in mutual funds. It consists of investing a fixed amount in a fund at regular intervals. When you invest the same amount, you buy fewer shares when the fund's price is relatively high and more shares when it is low. The advantage of this method is that it reduces the average cost per share during the investment period.

In comparison, DCAP is a refinement on typical dollar-cost averaging. With the typical method, the amount you invest, whether monthly, quarterly, yearly, or at other intervals, is fixed. DCAP requires that you invest each month, and the amount of your investment should vary in relation to a target price.

DCAP assumes that the trend of most mutual fund prices is up, but there will be both up and down price fluctuations as prices rise. To profit from these fluctuations, DCAP requires that you set a target price to control the amount of your monthly investment. If your fund's price, the net asset value (NAV), drops below the target price, you increase your monthly investment. If your fund's price is equal to or higher than the target price, you continue to invest the same amount.

In many ways DCAP is similar to typical dollar-cost averaging, but there are differences:

* The DCAP formula requires monthly investments, while typical dollar-cost averaging investments can be monthly, quarterly, yearly, or at other intervals.

* The amount of DCAP investments can vary, but the amount of typical dollar-cost averaging investments are fixed.

* DCAP requires the setting of a target price to determine the amount of each investment. Typical dollar-cost averaging does not require a target price.

DCAP'S Components

When you use the DCAP formula, there are four components to consider:

* Your initial investment.

* A target price.

* Your maximum investment.

* The amount of your monthly investment.

To see how the formula's components function, let's create an imaginary fund. We'll assume that you want to invest in an IRA to supplement your retirement income. You select XYZ Growth Fund because it holds quality growth stocks, appears well-managed, and has an average annual return of 18 percent for the last five years. What's more, after you satisfy the fund's initial investment requirement of $500, you decide to invest a minimum of $100 each month. Here's a rundown of DCAP's components and how they function in relation to your investments in XYZ Fund selling at $20 a share.

Initial investment

Your initial investment of $500 at $20 a share buys 25.000 shares in XYZ Fund. (The number of shares in mutual fund transactions is carried to three decimal places, which accounts for your fractional ownership of shares).

Target price

To set the target price, let's assume that during the past five years the trading range of XYZ Fund was from a high of $22 to a low of $17. Since you feel that $20 is a fair price for the fund, you set that figure as the target price.

Maximum investment

Each 5 percent drop in XYZ's price below the target price requires that you increase your investment 20 percent, but only to a maximum of 100 percent. A 100 percent increase in your investment correlates to a 25 percent drop in XYZ's price and that large a decrease could indicate the fund has a problem. If the fund drops 25 percent, it's better to stop investing and put your money, if only temporarily, in a money market fund.

Monthly investment amount

As long as the price of XYZ Fund sells above the $20 target price, your monthly investment will be $100. Your investment will exceed $100 only if XYZ's price drops below the $20 target price.

The table on the opposite page (Table 7-1) provides an easy way to determine the amount of your monthly investment in relation to price changes in XYZ Fund. Later in this chapter, under the heading "How the DCAP Formula Works," there is a more precise method to determine the amount to invest.

In the Monthly Investment Table the amount of your investment varies in relation to the change in XYZ's price from the target price. For example, when XYZ's price is $18, your investment is $140. At $17, it is $160. During the investment period, XYZ's target price remained at $20. If you feel the target price is too high or too low, reset it using one of the other methods explained later in this chapter.

The minimum monthly investment in the table is $100. If you decide to set your minimum at $50, divide the last column in the Monthly Investment Table by two and the result is the amount of your investment. For instance, if your fund's price is $17 (a 15 percent drop from your target price), your monthly investment is $80. The main idea of the DCAP formula is the percent of increase or decrease of each investment, not the minimum amount you decide to invest each month.

All figures in the Monthly Investment Table are rounded to the nearest dollar for simplicity. If the price of XYZ Fund is $19.50, for example, round it down to $19 as the basis for your investment. Similarly, if the fund's price is $19.51, round it up to $20.

MONTHLY INVESTMENT TABLE
XYZ FUND

Target price	Fund's price per share	Percent fund incr. decr. from target price	Percent increase in monthly investment	Monthly investment amount
$20	$20	-0-	-0-	$100
$20	$19	-5	20	$120
$20	$18	-10	40	$140
$20	$17	-15	60	$160
$20	$16	-20	80	$180
$20	$15	-25	100	$200
$20	$16	-20	80	$180
$20	$17	-15	60	$160
$20	$18	-10	40	$140
$20	$19	-5	20	$120
$20	$20	-0-	-0-	$100
$20	$20	-0-	-0-	$100

Table 7-1

THE TARGET PRICE

The target price determines the amount of your monthly investment. It is a trigger mechanism that rises or falls in relation to the price of your fund. When accurately set, it could greatly increase the value of your fund.

To see how the target price functions, let's assume that you open an IRA account with a fund at $20 a share. Further, let's suppose you feel the fund's price of $20 is a good target price to determine the amount of your future investments of at least $100 a month.

If the price of your fund drops to $19 (a 5 percent decrease), you increase the amount of your monthly investment by 20 percent, to $120. Similarly, if the price drops to $18 (a 10 percent decrease from the target price), you increase your investment 40 percent, to $140. If the fund's price then rises from $18 to $20 (the target price), your monthly investment would decrease from $140 to $100. So each 5 percent drop in your fund below the target price requires a 20 percent increase in your investment, to a total of 100 percent. And each 5 percent return toward the target price requires a 20 percent decrease in your investment.

The minimum amount of the monthly investment used in this example is $100. Naturally, your minimum could be greater or less than $100. The amount should be what you can afford and still meet the minimum requirements of the fund.

SETTING THE TARGET PRICE

After you make your initial investment in a fund, set the target price. There are many methods you can use to determine the price. Here are some of the methods:

Initial cost per share

One method is to set the target price at the initial cost per share when you open an account with a fund. If your initial cost is $20, set the target price at $20. When you use your initial cost per share as the target price, you assume that the fund is fairly valued at that price.

Median price of fund

Another method is to set the target price in relation to the high/low price range of your fund for the past year or multiple of years.

If the high/low range of your fund for the previous year was from $20 to $16, for example, set the target price at $18, the median price. If the range was from $20 to $14, set the target price at $17, also the median price.

The median price for a five to ten year period, that covers both up and down market cycles, should provide a more reliable account of a fund's volatility and a more accurate target price. Let's say, for example, your fund's high/low range was from $24 to $16 for the last five years, and you choose that period to set the target price. In this case, the target price is set at $20.

Stock market indexes

You could set the target price in relation to a market index. There are several indexes that measure stock market performance. The most widely referenced indexes are the Dow Jones Industrial Average, Standard and Poor's 500 (S&P 500), and the NASDAQ (National Association of Securities Dealers Automated Quotation System).

Let's suppose that you select the Dow Jones Industrial Average for the past year to set your target price. If the Dow Jones is 20 percent below its high price for the past year, set your target price 20 percent below your fund's high price for that period. Similarly, if you select the S&P 500 or the NASDAQ, set the target price the same percentage as the index is below its high price.

Selecting an index

Before you select a market index to set the target price, review your fund's prospectus to determine which exchange lists most of the fund's stocks. Then select that exchange to set the target price. If most of the stocks in your fund are listed on the NASDAQ Exchange, for example, choose that exchange to set the target price.

There are several ways to set the target price and none of them are perfect. They are merely methods you can use to determine the amount of your monthly investment. Of the methods listed, the more accurate one probably is the median price of your fund for the past few years. This assumes that your fund has been in operation for the period you select.

How The DCAP Formula Works

Now that you are familiar with DCAP's components, let's look at the DCAP formula. To make the formula easy to apply, these alpha designations are used:

A = Target price
B = Fund price
C = Target price less fund price
D = 20 percent variance multiplier
E = Monthly investment increase/decrease
F = Minimum monthly investment
G = Total monthly investment

DCAP formula: A - B = C   C can not be less than 0

$$C \times D = E$$
$$E + F = G$$

The following is an example of how the DCAP formula works. The fund's trading range is $22 to $18, the target price set at $20, and the minimum monthly investment is $100.

DCAP Formula						
A - B = C ; C x D = E ; E + F = G						
Target Price	Fund Price	Target Price Less Fund Price	Times 20% Variance	Monthly Investment Inc./Dec.	Minimum Monthly Investment	Total Monthly Investment
$20.00	$20.00	-0-	20	-0-	$100	$100
$20.00	$18.55	$1.45	20	$29	$100	$129
$20.00	$18.09	$1.91	20	$38	$100	$138
$20.00	$17.52	$2.48	20	$50	$100	$150
$20.00	$17.20	$2.80	20	$56	$100	$156
$20.00	$16.94	$3.06	20	$61	$100	$161
$20.00	$17.44	$2.56	20	$51	$100	$151
$20.00	$18.28	$1.72	20	$34	$100	$134
$20.00	$18.72	$1.28	20	$26	$100	$126
$20.00	$19.50	$0.50	20	$10	$100	$110
$20.00	$20.00	-0-	20	-0-	$100	$100
$20.00	$22.09	-0-	20	-0-	$100	$100
Totals				$355	$1,200	$1,555

Table 7-2

In the example, the target price remained at $20 during the 12-month investment period. When the fund's price fell below the target price, the difference was multiplied by a 20 percent variance to arrive at the increase or decrease in the amount of the monthly investment.

Any increase in the monthly investment is added to the minimum of $100 to determine the total investment. The minimum investment could be higher or lower than $100 and the formula would not change.

RESETTING THE TARGET PRICE

There is good advice in the saying "if it works don't fix it." You can apply the same reasoning to your fund's target price. There are only three reasons for you to reset the target price: when you set it in relation to the high/low price of your fund and your fund sets a new high price; when you set it in relation to one of the market indexes and the index sets a new high price; and if your fund makes a distribution. If you invest in your fund for the longer term, say 10 to 15 years, you may have to reset the target price only a few times during that period.

Resetting the target price for new highs

If you set the target price in relation to your fund's price and the fund rises to a new high, reset the target price. For example, suppose you invest in a fund with a price range from $24 to $20 you set the target price at $22 and a few months later the fund sets a new high price of $25. In this case, reset the target price at $22.50, the median price. You can apply the same methodology when you use the Dow Jones, S&P 500, and the NASDAQ indexes as a reference to set the target price.

Resetting the target price for distributions

There are two ways you can receive distributions from your fund: dividends and capital gains. When your fund makes a distribution, you will receive a statement from the fund that shows the date and dollar amount distributed, number of new shares purchased (if you reinvest your distribution in the fund), purchase price of the new shares, and the total shares you own.

Since distributions reduce a fund's assets, the price of a fund is adjusted downward to reflect its new value. For instance, a fund's price that is $21 the day before a $0.50 distribution will decrease to $20.50 after the distribution. Because the securities held by the fund may increase or decrease in value the day of the distribution, they also must figure into the new price of the fund.

Taking the above example a step further, suppose the securities held by your fund fell $0.50 on the distribution date. In that case, the new price of the fund is $20. You arrive at $20 by deducting $0.50 for the distribution and $0.50 for the decrease in the securities held by the fund from $21.

Let's look at the above example again and assume that your fund's trading range is $23 to $16 before the distribution, with a $20 target price. Since the fund did not drop below the $20 target price on the date of the distribution, the target price is not reset.

Only when a distribution, with an increase or decrease in the fund's price that changes the trading range, is the target price reset. When you reset the target price after a distribution, it is usually to a lower figure and may require an increase in your monthly investment.

Resetting the target price for a new low after a distribution

To set the target price for a new low after a distribution, let's say the price of your fund is $20, the trading range is from $21 to $19, and the target price is $20. Your fund then declares a $1.50 distribution, and on the distribution date the fund drops $0.50 in value. In this case, your fund has set a new low and the new trading range is $21 to $18. The target price is then reset to $19.50 and would require a $30 increase in your monthly investment if your minimum is $100.

Here's an example of how to determine the target price and amount to invest if your fund sets a new low after a distribution.

Pre-distribution:

Trading range of fund	$21-$19
Price of fund	$20
Target price	$20
Amount of monthly investment	$100
Amount of distribution	$1.50
Increase or decrease in fund's price on the distribution date	$0.50

Post-distribution:

Trading range of fund	$21-$18

($1.50 plus $0.50 = $2 deducted from pre-distribution fund price of $20)

Price of fund ($20 less $2)	$18
Target price	$19.50
Amount of monthly investment	$130

(new target price of $19.50 less new fund price of $18 = $1.50 x 20 percent variance = $130)

Resetting the target price for a new high after a distribution

Only rarely will a fund set a new high price after a distribution. If a new high does occur on that date, the target price should be reset to reflect the fund's new trading range.

Let's suppose that your fund's trading range is $20 to $18, the target price is $19, and the current price of the fund is $19.50. The fund makes a $0.25 distribution and its price rises $1 on the same date.

In this situation, the fund set a new high at $20.25 so the new target price is $19.12. You determine the new target price by adding the $1 increase in the fund's price to $19.50 and deducting the $0.25 distribution. Next, total the fund's high price ($20.25) and low price ($18) then divide by two to get $19.12. The initial setting and then resetting of the target price is the key to greater profits when you use the DCAP formula. Be sure to examine the target price before each monthly investment, after distributions, and when your fund sets a new high price.

DCAP COMPARED TO TYPICAL DOLLAR-COST AVERAGING

Any new investment strategy should prove that it is better than existing ways of investing. To see how investing by the DCAP formula compares with that of typical dollar-cost averaging, let's invest in three imaginary funds.

We'll name the funds A, B, and C. The investments in Fund A are consistent with the DCAP formula, while investments in Fund B are monthly and Fund C semiannually, both in accord with typical dollar-cost averaging. Funds B and C have no target price, but Fund A has a $20 target price that remains fixed during the investment period. So if Fund A's price drops below $20, the amount of the monthly investment increases

FUND A
DOLLAR-COST AVERAGING PLUS

Date of Investment	Cost per Share	Dollar Amount of Investment	No. Shares Bought	Cummulative Shares
January	$20	$500*	25.000	25.000
February	$21	$100	4.761	29.761
March	$18	$140	7.777	37.538
April	$17	$160	9.411	46.949
May	$16	$180	11.250	58.199
June	$15	$200	13.333	71.532
July	$17	$160	9.411	80.943
August	$18	$140	7.777	88.720
September	$19	$120	6.315	95.035
October	$20	$100	5.000	100.035
November	$21	$100	4.761	104.796
December	$22	$100	4.545	109.341
Totals		$2,000	109.341	109.341

Value of Fund A in December $2,405
  (109.341 shares times $22)
Amount invested $2,000
Amount of gain or (loss) $ 405
Rate of return   20.25 percent
  ($405 divided by $2,000)

* Initial investment of $500. Table excludes capital gain and dividend distributions

Table 7-3

Fund B
Typical Dollar-Cost Averaging
Monthly Investments

Date of Investment	Cost per Share	Dollar Amount of Investment	No. Shares Bought	Cummulative Shares
January	$20	$500*	25.000	25.000
February	$21	$100	4.761	29.761
March	$18	$100	5.555	35.316
April	$17	$100	5.882	41.198
May	$16	$100	6.250	47.448
June	$15	$100	6.666	54.114
July	$17	$100	5.882	59.996
August	$18	$100	5.555	65.551
September	$19	$100	5.263	70.814
October	$20	$100	5.000	75.814
November	$21	$100	4.761	80.575
December	$22	$100	4.545	85.120
Totals		$1,600	85.120	85.120

Value of Fund B in December	$1,872
(85.120 shares times $22)	
Amount invested	$1,600
Amount of gain or (loss)	$ 272
Rate of return	17 percent
($272 divided by $1,600)	

* Initial investment of $500. Table excludes capital gain and dividend distributions

Table 7-4

When you compare the three funds, there's no question that DCAP (Fund A) provides a greater return than typical dollar-cost averaging. The return on Fund A is 20.25 percent, Fund B 17 percent, and 4.93 percent on Fund C. A difference of around 15 percent between the return on Funds A and C, is too large a figure to go unnoticed. Even the difference of 3.25 percent between the return on Funds A and B is significant when the percentage is compounded for several years.

The initial investment in Funds A and B was $500. Later investments in Fund A were in accord with the DCAP formula's target price and ranged from $100 to $200 a month. Investments in Fund B were constant at $100 a month.

FUND C
TYPICAL DOLLAR-COST AVERAGING
SEMIANNUALLY INVESTMENTS

Date of Investment	Cost per Share	Dollar Amount of Investment	No. Shares Bought	Cummulative Shares
January	$20	$800*	40.000	40.000
December	$22	$800	36.363	76.363
Totals		$1,600	76.363	76.363

Value of Fund C in December	$1,679
(76.363 shares times $22)	
Amount invested	$1,600
Amount of gain or (loss)	$ 79
Rate of return	4.93 percent
($79 divided by $1,600)	

* Initial investment of $800. Table excludes capital gain and dividend distributions.

Table 7-5

In Fund C there were two investments, $800 in January and $800 in December. The return on this fund was a low 4.93 percent because one-half ($800) of the total investment was made in January when the fund was at its highest price.

Remember, all three funds are hypothetical and contain arbitrary figures. So there is no guarantee that you can earn 20.25 percent or even 4.93 percent when you invest in a fund. Yet, when you review the figures on many funds a 20 percent return or even higher is possible.

DCAP RESERVE FUND

It's a good idea to have a reserve fund when you use the DCAP formula. A reserve fund serves two purposes: to provide money when the DCAP formula requires that you increase your investment in a fund; and to have money available for emergencies. If your mutual fund is part of a family of funds, there's usually a money market fund available for a reserve fund.

When you use the DCAP formula, monthly investments stop if your fund drops 25 percent in price. Should this occur, a reserve fund is a convenient place to invest the money destined for your fund. The idea here is to keep in the habit of investing monthly. Later, when you decide whether to continue with the same fund or switch to another, you can reinvest the money.

Chapter 8

Building A Retirement Portfolio

It's always possible to have a financially secure retirement. What's required is to build a retirement portfolio that will provide additional retirement income.

Contrary to what some people believe, there is no mystery to building a retirement portfolio. It is merely a group of three or four investments held for a specific goal -to supplement the income you receive from your retirement plan at work.

A retirement portfolio should be designed to offset riskier investments with safer ones, and offset investments in one area with investments in other areas. Deciding which investments are best for you involves two decisions: One, is the risk level acceptable? And two, which kind of investments are the best? Clearly, the risks involved with collectibles, gold and silver bullion, numismatic (rare) coins, commodity contracts, limited partnerships, and collateralized mortgage obligations make them unacceptable for most people.

Less risky investments include mutual funds, stocks, bonds, and money market funds. For example, your portfolio could contain two mutual funds, three stocks, two municipal bonds and a money market fund with a total value of $120,000.

No portfolio will be the same for all families or all individuals. And there is no magic formula for building your portfolio; however, there are some general rules of thumb, starting with the safety of your principal.

Safety Of Principal

When it comes to your portfolio, the first concern should be the safety of your principal — the protection of your original investment. Put another way, the first step in making money is not to lose it. Clearly, if you don't lose money, you've done nothing more than break even.

Not surprisingly, safety of principal is inconsistent with a high return on an investment. If you want a relatively good return, you must take some risk and accept the likelihood of losing some of your money. You can usually earn a good return if you avoid speculative investments and those you don't fully understand.

RISK

All investments involve risk — the chance that you may lose all or part of your money. Risk applies not only to the safety of your principal but also to the return on your investment. This means you can have a relatively safe investment and yet be susceptible to risk because of what an investment earns through interest, dividends, and capital gains.

Since you cannot avoid risk when you invest, you need to find a way to manage it. So, before you select an investment, determine your risk level. The table below lists several investments by their risk and potential return. Review the investments and decide which ones are within your comfort zone.

RELATIVE RISK AND RETURN RANKINGS		
TYPE OF INVESTMENT	RISK LEVEL	POTENTIAL RETURN
Government securities	Low	Medium
Municipal bonds	Low	Medium
Bank instruments	Medium	Low
Annuities	Medium	Low
Money market mutual funds	Medium	Medium
Corporate bonds	Medium	Medium
Bond mutual funds	Medium	Medium
Growth mutual funds	Medium	High
Quality growth stocks	Medium/High	High
Zero-coupon bonds	Medium/High	High
Rental real estate	Medium	Medium
Limited partnerships	High	Medium
Numismatic coins	High	Medium
Commodity contracts	High	High
Futures contracts	High	High

Table 8-1

The level of risk and potential return assigned to the investments in the table could vary according to who did the ranking, but there is a general consensus on those investments that are placed at the top and bottom of the table.

Don't let risk be the only factor when you select an investment. Weigh the risk of an investment against its potential return, then consider only those within your comfort zone.

DIVERSIFICATION

Diversification is an investment strategy for reducing risk. It is best described as not putting all your eggs in one basket. In truth, it is the foundation of any well-structured portfolio.

Since all investments carry a degree of risk, one way to reduce it is to diversify your portfolio by holding a combination of mutual funds, stocks, bonds, and money market funds. The proper mix depends on your age, family needs, and retirement expectations. Even if you have only a small amount to invest, apportion it among several investments to reduce your risk.

When you invest in a stock mutual fund, you get immediate diversification. That's because a stock fund holds securities such as stocks, bonds, and cash equivalents. If you also invest in bond and money market funds, your portfolio is even more diversified and less risky.

Diversification does not mean to invest in as many different types of securities as possible, but to select a few that meet your goals, expected return, and risk level.

DEVELOPING YOUR PORTFOLIO

The basic building blocks for your retirement portfolio are stocks, bonds, and mutual funds. You can invest in stocks and bonds individually or in mutual funds.

Stocks have the potential to provide the greatest return and offer the best chance of beating inflation. Bonds won't provide much protection against inflation since they pay a fixed rate of return. Yet, bonds usually prosper when the economy is weak. Mutual funds meet the needs of many investors. They are easy to acquire and over the long haul many funds have provided some attractive returns.

If you are relatively young with a promising career and good prospects for steady income growth, you could hold more speculative investments. In this case, your portfolio might include a high percent of growth stocks or a growth stock fund; medium grade corporate bonds or a corporate bond fund; and a money market fund. Your portfolio should be flexible enough so you can modify your asset mix when your goals and family needs change.

If you are near retirement age and you want to preserve your money, then your portfolio should be relatively conservative. It might include a corporate bond fund, quality common stocks, growth mutual fund, and a money market fund — a balanced portfolio. Remember, the closer you are to retirement the less time you'll have to make up for investments that fail.

Regardless of your investment mix, it's wise to have a money market fund for emergencies. A money market fund provides a cushion so you won't have to sell your investments to raise cash for an unexpected emergency.

PORTFOLIO INVESTMENTS

In addition to mutual funds, which were covered in Chapter 6, there's an assortment of investments to supplement your retirement income and new ones are appearing almost every day. Since many of the newer investments have not shown they can provide a good return and their safety is questionable, it's probably better to consider only those that have a proven performance record. The list of investments that follows includes most of the popular ones, each with its own degree of risk and potential return.

Government securities

The federal government offers a variety of debt securities. Many are exempt from state and local taxes, but subject to federal taxes. They are probably the safest investments available and offer an array of yields and maturity dates. The more available government securities include treasury bills, notes, and bonds.

Treasury bills are short-term investments that mature in 13, 26, and 52 weeks. They are auctioned each week and sell at a discount to their par value of $10,000. If you don't have $10,000, less the discount, forget about treasury bills.

Treasury notes mature in two to ten years. Some notes sell in denominations of $1,000 and mature in four years or more. Others require a minimum of $5,000 and mature earlier. The yield on treasury notes is comparable to the yield on treasury bills.

Treasury bonds are longer-term investments that mature in five to thirty years. Some treasury bonds can be called in (redeemed by the government) before their maturity date. They sell in denominations of $1,000 or more.

Federal agency securities

Federal agency securities are offered in $1,000 units or more by government agencies such as the Government National Mortgage Association, Student Loan Marketing Association, and federal land banks. They provide a greater yield to maturity than treasury securities, often a percentage point more. But federal agency securities, unlike treasury securities, have no government guarantee for the payment of interest and return of principal so they carry more risk.

Common stocks

If you are willing to assume the risk, common stocks could be a good investment to supplement your retirement income. Through the years, stocks have provided a greater return than all other types of investments.

If you invest in stocks, first decide which type to buy. Do you want blue chip, growth, income, cyclical, speculative, or defensive stocks? Next, determine how much to invest in stocks. If you are uncomfortable with risk, then only a small percent of your money should be in stocks.

There are quality stocks in most every industry. These are the leading industry stocks with sales and earnings that increase most every year. They usually offer products or services with growth potential, pay dividends, and emphasize the development of new products or services. Their management is usually aggressive and experienced. These are the types of stocks to consider.

Corporate bonds

When you purchase a corporate bond, you are lending money to the corporation that issued the bond. You have no ownership in the corporation. Instead, the issuing corporation agrees to pay you a fixed rate of interest, usually semiannually, until the bond matures. Upon maturity, the corporation redeems the bond at face value.

Corporate bonds are usually issued in denominations of $1,000 or more and their market price is listed daily in most large newspapers. Because a bond's interest rate is fixed, its price will vary to reflect prevailing interest rates.

Municipal bonds

Municipal, or tax-exempt bonds as they are often called, are issued by state and local governments. Most are general obligation bonds with interest paid by the taxing power of the issuer, or as revenue bonds with interest paid by a specific project such as a toll bridge or road. The most attractive aspect of municipal bonds is that their interest is exempt from federal income tax.

Whether the tax-exempt feature of a municipal bond is more favorable than a taxable bond depends on your income tax bracket and the yield of the bond. To decide whether a taxable or non- taxable bond provides the highest yield, determine your tax bracket and subtract it from 100, divide the result into the tax-exempt yield and the percent is equal to a taxable yield. For example, if you are in the 28 percent tax bracket, a 5 percent tax-exempt yield is equal to a 6.94 percent taxable yield. You should be aware that there are some risks to municipal bonds, since interest payments depend on the financial condition of the issuer.

Zero-coupon bonds

Zero-coupon bonds are debt securities that pay interest at maturity. They are issued in denominations as low as $1,000 and are sold at discount to their face value. For example, you might pay $205 for a zero-coupon bond that yields 9 percent and matures in 18 years. Zero-coupons are usually good investments because their interest will accumulate until you withdraw the money, presumably when you retire. Thus, you can choose a maturity date to coincide with your retirement, and you'll know what your return will be at maturity. It's wise to buy zero-coupons no lower than those rated BBB by Standard and Poor's and Baa by Moody's.

Since corporate, municipal, and zero-coupon bonds have varying degrees of risk, there are companies that rate them according to their credit worthiness. Two of the more popular rating companies are Standard and Poor's and Moody's. The table below shows the bond ratings used by these companies. In addition to the ratings each company uses a qualifier: + or - by Standard and Poor's and 1,2, or 3 by Moody's.

BOND RATINGS

Standard and Poor's	Moody's	Bond Quality
AAA	Aaa	Highest quality
AA	Aa	High quality
A	A	Good quality
BBB	Baa	Medium grade
BB	Ba	Speculative, some defensive qualities
B	B	Highly speculative
CCC	Caa	Bonds not paying interest or in default
CC	Ca	Lowest rating
C	C	
D		

Table 8-2

Those bonds rated AAA by Standard & Poor's and Aaa by Moody's are considered the least risky. The investment grade bonds are those rated no lower than BBB by Standard and Poor's and Baa by Moody's. The bonds of telephone, gas, and electric utility companies usually carry one of the highest ratings.

Series EE Savings Bonds

These bonds (originally named Series E Savings Bonds) come in denominations of $50 to $10,000 and are sold at a discount to their face value. There is no sales charge when you buy them, and there is a guaranteed minimum rate, tied to the return on treasury securities, if you hold them for at least five years.

Series EE Bonds are exempt from state and local taxes, but subject to federal tax. They are a safe investment with an average yield, and you could consider them for your retirement portfolio.

Money Market Mutual Funds

Although not insured by the federal government, money market funds are one of the safest investments available. Aside from their safety, they are a useful investment for your retirement portfolio.

You can make deposits to and withdrawals from a money market fund at any time and the fund takes care of the recordkeeping. You receive regular statements from the fund that show all transactions and a year-end summary for tax purposes. The shares of most money market funds are sold and redeemed without charge. Here are some of the advantages that a money market mutual fund can offer:

* A parking place between financial transactions until you decide where to invest your money.

* A cash account for bill paying.

* An investment that provides a "fair" yield.

* A source of tax-free income when you invest in a tax-exempt money market fund.

* An emergency fund.

MODEL PORTFOLIOS

Building your retirement portfolio is not complicated. However, it will need monitoring and careful management, but not frequent changes. How you build and manage your portfolio will depend on your investment time horizon, your risk level, and any changes in your plans for retirement.

As it turns out, the five model portfolios listed below will not fit everyone's investment needs. Among the portfolios, there can be considerable overlapping and different asset mixes. As you approach retirement, for example, you may want a larger percent of your money in bonds and less in common stocks. Even so, the models will show you how to build a retirement portfolio.

PORTFOLIO #1

Age Group	Type of Investment	Percent of Total Portfolio
20s	Corporate bond fund	25 percent
	Growth stock fund	25 percent
	Money market fund	50 percent
		100 percent

Portfolio #1 is a conservative portfolio intended primarily for the beginning investor, usually someone just out of high school or college. The portfolio has the potential to provide a good total return by including a growth fund. Yet 50 percent is invested in a money market fund as a reserve for emergencies and future investments.

PORTFOLIO #2

Age Group	Type of Investment	Percent of Total Portfolio
30s	Corporate bond fund	25 percent
	Growth stock fund	25 percent
	Common stocks	25 percent
	Money market fund	25 percent
		100 percent

Portfolio #2 is designed for the moderately conservative investor who is raising a family, but feels it's time to start buying common stocks to supplement retirement income. The money market fund is reduced from the 50 percent allocation in Portfolio #1 to 25 percent to buy stocks.

74   Lyle Allen
Portfolio #3

Age Group	Type of Investment	Percent of Total Portfolio
40s	Corporate bond fund	25 percent
	Growth stock fund	25 percent
	Common stocks	35 percent
	Money market fund	15 percent
		100 percent

Portfolio #3 is for the investor whose children are completing college and no longer need financial support. By now, the investor has well-defined goals and enough experience and confidence to take a more aggressive investment approach. The money market fund in Portfolio #2 is reduced 10 percent to increase the percentage of common stocks in Portfolio #3.

Portfolio #4

Age Group	Type of Investment	Percent of Total Portfolio
50s	Corporate bond fund	15 percent
	Municipal bond fund	15 percent
	Growth stock fund	25 percent
	Common stocks	35 percent
	Money market fund	10 percent
		100 percent

Portfolio #4 is more suitable for investors during their peak earning years. The percent in common stocks remains the same as Portfolio #3, but the money market fund is reduced 5 percent and corporate bond fund 10 percent to buy tax-free bonds to offset taxable income.

Portfolio #5

Age Group	Type of Investment	Percent of Total Portfolio
60s+	Corporate bond fund	15 percent
	Municipal bond fund	15 percent
	Growth stock fund	25 percent
	Common stocks	25 percent
	Money market fund	20 percent
		100 percent

Portfolio #5 is for the investor nearing or in retirement. Except for Portfolio #1, Portfolio #5 is the most conservative of all the portfolios. The percent in corporate and municipal bond funds is the same as Portfolio #4, while stocks are reduced 10 percent and added to the money market fund for emergency situations.

MAKING YOUR MONEY GROW

One way to make your money grow is through the compounding of interest, dividends, and capital gain distributions that your portfolio produces. This means all distributions, and the money produced by them, are continuously working for you to provide maximum growth. This is achieved by reinvesting the distributions generated by your portfolio rather than receiving them in cash.

Another way to maximize money growth is to make regular additions to your portfolio. You can do this by requesting your employer to deduct money from your salary and send it to a mutual fund, or asking your bank to send money from your checking account to a fund.

Finally, you can defer taxes to achieve growth. The most obvious way to postpone taxes is to contribute to the retirement plan where you work. If there is no plan at work, open an IRA. If you are self-employed, start a Keogh Plan.

PORTFOLIO CHECKUP

Just as a motor tuneup can keep your car in good running condition, a review of your portfolio can keep it in shape. But remember, a review of your portfolio doesn't mean it has to be completely overhauled.

It's a good practice to check the price of a mutual fund before each investment. When you use the DCAP formula, you'll need to know the fund's price to determine the amount of your next investment. Most large newspapers carry the price of funds. What's more, after each investment, your fund will send you a statement that shows the number of shares purchased, the purchase price, and the total shares you own. The statement includes enough information to check your fund's performance.

Since stocks carry more risk than mutual funds, it's a good idea to check them daily. Any 10 percent drop in the price of a stock is cause for concern, and you should determine the reason for the decline.

Once you gather the information about your portfolio, what do you do with it? First, compare the return on your investments with similar types of investments. For example, compare the performance of your mutual funds with that of the S&P 500 or another market index. Next, compare the return on your money market mutual fund with a money market deposit account at a bank. In short, compare your portfolio's performance on an individual and overall return basis with similar investments. If your return is less than comparable investments, maybe it's time to change your portfolio mix.

Part Three
PREPARING FOR
RETIREMENT

Not to know is bad; not
to wish to know is worse.

-African proverb

Chapter 9

SAVING FOR RETIREMENT

Many people spend nearly all of their lives earning money and looking forward to retirement. But when the time comes to retire, they only have enough to pay their monthly bills. What goes wrong? Why are there people whose only chance for a wealthy retirement is to win the lottery? Their misfortune is easy to explain -they didn't save for their retirement.

The starting point for retirement savings begins with your cash flow. Once you can control your cash flow, you not only find ways to save but you also develop good spending habits.

CASH FLOW

Cash flow is the term that describes the movement of money into and from your financial accounts. You can determine your cash flow by showing how much money went in and out of your accounts during a certain period.

It doesn't matter whether you are a one or multi-person family, you can determine your cash flow. It's usually better to look at cash flow on a monthly basis, even if you are paid weekly or biweekly. That's because a frequent review is time consuming and many expenses such as housing, auto, and utility payments are due monthly. You'll find that some of your expenses, like housing and auto payments are a fixed amount, while others, such as food, clothing, education, recreation, and transportation, can vary by month.

The way to look at your cash flow is to complete a cash flow worksheet. When you finish the worksheet below, you'll know the sources of your income, where your income is spent, and should get some ideas on ways to save money for retirement.

One benefit of the cash flow worksheet is that it shows where your money comes from, where it goes, and how much is available for retirement savings.

Another benefit of the cash flow worksheet is that it allows you to look at your living expenses and decide if you can reduce them. A good way to view your living

Cash Flow Worksheet

Month _____ 19 _____

INCOME SOURCES

Salary/wages $_____
Investment income $_____
Other $_____

Total income $_____

EXPENSES

Mortgage/rent $_____
Utilities (electric, gas, water, garbage, phone) $_____
Food (grocery stores, restaurants) $_____
Insurance (life, health, auto, housing) $_____
Medical (not covered by insurance) $_____
Taxes (property/income) $_____
Auto payments $_____
Education $_____
Clothing $_____
Gifts/contributions $_____
Subscriptions (books, magazines) $_____
Membership dues $_____
Vacations/entertainment $_____
Personal care $_____
Transportation $_____
Credit cards $_____
Other $_____

Total expenses $_____

RESULTS:

Total income $_____
Less total expenses $_____
Money available for savings $_____

expenses is to realize that every dollar saved in the expense category goes directly to the bottom line, your cash flow. Chapter 10 suggests several ways you can reduce your living expenses.

It's a good idea to complete a 12-month cash flow worksheet to see which months have the highest expenses. With a yearly review, you'll get a better picture of your cash flow. As a rule, you'll find that your expenses are higher in those months when there are back-to-school outlays, gifts to buy, and vacation costs.

SAVINGS PLANS

A review of your cash flow would be incomplete without a plan for saving money. The advantage of a savings plan is that it gets you in the habit of setting aside part of your income for retirement.

There's no doubt that the way a family saves money is affected by factors such as age, education, sex, and amount of income. Regardless of what factors might affect your savings outlook, a wealthy retirement depends on your ability to save money. Two of the best ways to set aside some savings are to save a percent or a part of your income.

Saving a percent of your income

A realistic and meaningful amount to save each month is 10 percent of your gross income. As it turns out, you don't have to set aside 10 percent as soon as you start a savings plan. Begin slow, save 2 percent the first three months, then increase the amount you save every three months by 2 percent. At the end of fifteen months, you should be able to save 10 percent of your income. It works like this:

SAVINGS SCHEDULE

Monthly percent to save	Number of months to save
2	3
4	3
6	3
8	3
10	3
Goal: 10 percent	Total months = 15

Saving a part of your income

Another way to save is to set aside a dollar amount of your income. You could, for example, make regular deposits from your paycheck to a money market mutual fund, bank, savings and loan, or credit union account, although this method is not as good as saving a percent of your income.

The advantage of saving a percent rather than a dollar amount of your income is that presumably your savings will keep pace with inflation. This means that higher rates of inflation may be accompanied with increases in your income and a higher return on your savings.

SAVINGS GROWTH

Once you start a savings plan, its growth will depend on how much you contribute. The following are projections on the amount you will have to save each year to achieve a savings goal of $10,000 at 5, 8, and 10 percent rates of return.

YEARLY SAVINGS TO ACCUMULATE $10,000

	RATE OF RETURN		
Number of years to save	5%	8%	10%
3	$3,174	$3,076	$3,021
5	$1,808	$1,703	$1,639
7	$1,228	$1,121	$1,053

The projections show that you can accumulate $10,000 in three years if you save $3,174 a year and earn 5 percent on your money. In five years, at 8 percent, you'll need to set aside $1,703 to save $10,000.

At first glance, it may seem impossible to save $10,000 in five years. But the good point about a savings plan is that you don't have to do it all at once. You save monthly, so it's easier than it appears. If you feel it's impossible to save $10,000 in five years, then half that amount and set a $5,000 savings goal.

STRATEGIES FOR SAVING MONEY

If you are just starting a savings plan, you may have to stretch your paycheck to cover monthly expenses. In this case, you should have a strategy for saving money. Once you have a strategy your savings plan will start to become a reality. The following are some strategies on how to save:

Pay yourself

After you pay your bills, what do you do with the money that's left? Sooner or later you will probably spend it, maybe on items you can do without. You can put that money to work by paying yourself. The idea of paying yourself is an often-used cliche, but very effective for saving money. Regardless of the cliche, one way to build savings is to set aside some money after you pay your monthly bills. It's only smart to run your financial affairs like a business by paying yourself.

Be a consistent saver

One of the ingredients found in most successful savings plans is consistency. Successful savers add money regularly to their savings. By doing so, their money grows not only because of their regular contributions, but also because of the compounding of their savings. When you can consistently save every month, it's surprising how quickly your savings will grow.

Give yourself a raise

When your employer gives you a raise, instead of spending the money increase the amount of your savings. By increasing the amount you save, your savings have a chance to stay ahead of inflation.

Treat your savings as untouchable

Savings must have time to grow. That means resisting the temptation to use money from your savings for day-to-day expenses. A payroll deduction to a money market fund or bank savings account is a good way to save because you don't actually handle the money. Since you don't receive the money, you reduce the chance that you'll spent it. The payoff comes when you have enough saved to live comfortably in retirement.

Chapter 10

REDUCING LIVING EXPENSES

When was the last time you thought about reducing your living expenses? It's easy to forget about cutting costs when there are other matters to attend to. Yet, when you can find ways to cut expenses, you'll have more money for retirement savings.

All families have major expenses. These include items such as mortgage or rent, insurance, and auto payments. These are fixed expenses and in many cases difficult to reduce. Other expense items such as utilities, food, clothing, vacations, and entertainment you can reduce more easily.

Look at the expenses you listed on the cash flow worksheet in Chapter 9 and decide how they can be reduced. Here are some ideas to get you started:

HOUSING

* If the interest rate on your house mortgage is higher than prevailing rates, see if you can refinance your mortgage. On a $100,000 mortgage, a 2 percent drop in your interest rate can save you about $140 a month.

* Consider extending the length of your mortgage, For example, extend a twenty-five year mortgage to thirty to reduce payments.

* Check with whoever holds your mortgage to see if your escrow account has excess money that you could withdraw.

AUTO PAYMENTS

* If you borrow money to buy an auto, check with more than one bank or credit union to get the lowest possible loan rate.

* Since you cannot deduct interest on an auto loan from your taxes, it's better to pay cash. If that isn't possible, consider buying a nearly

new rather than a new car after you have a mechanic check its condition. Many one-to two-year old cars have low mileage and are still under warranty.

INSURANCE

* Like many people, you may have more life insurance than you need. If you have children at home, the rule of thumb is a death benefit about seven times your annual income. Thus, if your income is $50,000, you'll need about $350,000 of insurance coverage. You can reduce your coverage to about three times your annual income if you have grown children. If you are single, $10,000 could be adequate.

* Health insurance is usually less costly when purchased under a group policy rather than individually. If you aren't eligible for group coverage, health maintenance organizations (HMOs) are one of the lower cost insurers.

* When it's time to renew your auto insurance, compare insurance rates from more than one company for the same coverage at less cost. Increase the deductible amount for collision insurance to reduce costs. Raising your deductible from $100 to $250 can reduce your yearly premium about 10 percent. And older cars usually don't need collision coverage if their value is below $3,000.

UTILITIES
Utilities are an area where you probably can make a substantial reduction. It could be possible to trim your utility costs by several hundred dollars. Here are some ideas:

* Caulk and weatherstrip the doors and windows on your house.

* Install an insulation blanket on your water heater. During the summer, set the thermostat on the water heater at 120 degrees or less. During winter, turn up the thermostat.

* Use ceiling fans to circulate the air in your house or apartment.

* Install shades and draperies to keep cold air outside and warm air inside.

* On your refrigerator, clean the coils, make sure the doors close tightly, and adjust the temperature for the season.

* Use a clothesline to dry clothes instead of an electric drier.

* Replace 100-watt light bulbs with 60-watt. Before you leave a room, turn off the lights.

* Make fewer long-distance telephone calls. Sign up for a special rate reduction program sponsored by most long-distance carriers. Make calls during those hours when rates are lower.

* Water your lawn and flowers at night. During daylight hours, much of the water evaporates.

FOOD
Here are some ways to cut your food costs:

* Shop for groceries at supermarkets or warehouse clubs where prices are usually lower than at convenience stores.

* Don't shop for groceries when you are hungry.

* Buy groceries less often to avoid impulse buying.

* Purchase staple groceries in bulk and store them to avoid inflationary pricing.

* Buy fresh fruits and vegetables only when they are in-season and less expensive.

* Buy generic brand food that usually costs less than name brands.

* When beef and poultry are on sale, buy them in bulk and store in your freezer.

* Use food discount coupons.

* Plant a vegetable garden.

GIFTS AND CONTRIBUTIONS

* Each January make a list of the people you plan to give gifts to during the year. Then buy gifts only when they are on sale.

* Avoid buying gifts a few days before Christmas when prices are usually higher.

* Wait until after the holidays, when the cost of many items is less, to buy next year's Christmas presents.

* Buy less expensive gifts.

* Consider carefully all your cash contributions to charities, especially if you cannot deduct donations from your income taxes.

EDUCATION

* Choose a public over a private school for your children's education.

* Buy school supplies off-season at discount stores or when they are on sale.

* Apply for college grants, loans, scholarships, and work-study programs.

CLOTHING

In the last few years, the dress code for many companies has changed. They no longer require all employees to wear suits and ties or dresses and high heels. More casual and comfortable clothing is now the policy. Here are some tips on buying clothing:

* Buy wash and wear clothes to save dry cleaning costs.

* Before you pay a high price for a tuxedo or formal dress that you may seldom wear, check the cost to rent them.

* Avoid buying clothes on impulse. Make up a clothing list when you shop and stick to it.

* Shop for clothes at designer outlets, off-price stores, and factory outlets where quality clothes usually cost less than at department stores.

* Buy clothes that coordinate your wardrobe. For example, purchase a sports jacket that goes with more than one pair of slacks and shoes you can wear with more than one dress.

TRANSPORTATION AND TRAVEL

* Take the subway, van pool, or ride the bus to and from work to cut your expenses. Driving your auto is usually more costly than using public transportation.

* Use no-fee travel checks, budget motels and hotels, airline discount fares, frequent flyer mileage, and compare prices when you travel.

* Long vacation trips can be costly. Instead of a two-week vacation away from home, limit your time to one week. Spend the second week on short, less costly, trips away from home.

These are some of the ways to reduce your living expenses. No doubt you can find other ways to cut expenses so that more of your income is available for retirement savings.

AN EXPENSE RECORD

One way to manage your money is to start a family expense record. An expense record is a guide to spending that will enable you to take control of your finances, live within your income, and set aside some savings.

An expense record can be exciting, challenging, and prove very profitable. All that's needed is to: first, account for what percent of your income goes for each expense item; and second, project what percent each expense item will be reduced. Once you become accustomed to accounting for your expenses, you'll probably find that it's not only easy to maintain but also that you can better manage your finances.

If you start an expense record, it's a good idea to involve all family members. Only when all members participate can you get good results. An expense record is useless if one family member follows the record and another goes on a spending spree. Before you start an expense record, here's a short quiz to see if you really need one:

* Do you have trouble paying your bills on time?

* If you have credit card debt, is the balance increasing or decreasing?

* Are you using cash advances on your credit cards for living expenses or to pay bills?

* Do you borrow money from friends or relatives to pay your bills?

* Do you put off saving money for your retirement?

* Do you draw from savings for daily expenses?

* Have you recently been denied credit?

If you answered yes to any of these questions, it's time to begin monthly (and yearly) expense records. Expense records are sometimes difficult to stick to and do require work, but they can provide some good results.

An expense record should contain an item to ensure there will be some monthly savings. If you don't include this item, there is the chance there will be none. Don't think that you can list expenses and generate savings as a residual. The best way to ensure there will be savings is probably to create a savings routine that you can live with. One way to do that is to have a savings deduction taken from your paycheck before you get a chance to spend it.

A problem with keeping an expense record concerns semi-annual or annual expenses that require adjustments. If all your expenses were due monthly and you were paid monthly, an expense record would be easy to maintain. Realistically, though, you might have to pay an insurance premium of $500 in June and another $500 in December. Thus, you'll have to set aside an amount each month so there will be money to meet the payments when due.

FAMILY EXPENSE RECORD

	Monthly or Yearly Cost	% of Total Cost	% of Planned Reductions
Essential Expenses			
Housing (mortgage, rent)	$_____	$_____	$_____
Utilities (electric, gas, gas, water, phone)	$_____	$_____	$_____
Food	$_____	$_____	$_____
Medical/dental	$_____	$_____	$_____
Insurance (life, health, auto, housing)	$_____	$_____	$_____
Taxes	$_____	$_____	$_____
Auto payments	$_____	$_____	$_____
Education	$_____	$_____	$_____
Savings	$_____	$_____	$_____
Other	$_____	$_____	$_____
Discretionary expenses			
Clothing	$_____	$_____	$_____
Personal care	$_____	$_____	$_____
Gifts/contributions	$_____	$_____	$_____
Subscriptions	$_____	$_____	$_____
Membership dues	$_____	$_____	$_____
Vacations/entertainment	$_____	$_____	$_____
Transportation	$_____	$_____	$_____
Credit cards	$_____	$_____	$_____
Other	$_____	$_____	$_____
Totals:	$_____	$100	$_____

Chapter 11

DEBT MANAGEMENT

We live in a nation of debtors, and borrowing money has replaced baseball as the national pastime. Getting in debt is as easy as buying tickets to a Minnesota Twins game. Getting out of debt is as difficult as trying to resell the same tickets.

There are several ways people get in debt. Most people use mortgage debt to buy a house and borrow to finance the purchase of an automobile. These are useful ways to purchase essential living needs. However, everything has a price and the price of borrowing money can be expensive. For example, the average American is carrying a balance of about $2,500 on credit cards and paying an average interest rate of 18 percent.

The trouble with debt is that it can get out of control and become a problem before many borrowers even realize it. The easiest way for debt to become a problem is probably with the excessive use of credit cards. Let's look at credit card debt to see how it can become a problem, and what you can do about it.

CREDIT CARDS

It's not news anymore that the excessive use of credit cards to pay for purchases is an easy way to get in debt. Credit card interest rates usually range from 12 to 21 percent. If you must borrow money on a credit card, use one that charges a low interest rate. The rates on some cards are around 12 to 13 percent. What's more, if your credit card issuer charges a high annual fee, switch to one with a lower fee. Consider any fee over $25 a year as high.

Credit card issuers make most of their money in two ways: they charge interest on what their customers borrow and they collect commissions from merchants. Both Visa and Master Card are owned by banks and collect commissions of about 2 percent on purchasers who use their cards.

In recent years, a new type of credit card has emerged: nonbank cards. These cards, issued by companies like General Motors, General Electric, and AT&T, offer a rebate toward the purchase of their goods or services. It's up to you to decide whether you are getting value by using a nonbank card.

If you have credit card debt, the following worksheet provides an easy way to determine whether it is under control. It will only take a few minutes to complete the worksheet and it could be worth the time spent.

CREDIT CARD WORKSHEET

Type of Credit Card	Amount Borrowed	Interest Rate	Outstanding Debit Balance	Monthly Payments
#1 _____	$_____	_____%	$_____	$_____
#2 _____	$_____	_____%	$_____	$_____
#3 _____	$_____	_____%	$_____	$_____
#4 _____	$_____	_____%	$_____	$_____
#5 _____	$_____	_____%	$_____	$_____
Totals	$_____	_____%	$_____	$_____

Appraisal:
(A) Monthly net income $_____
(B) Total monthly credit card payments $_____
(C) B divided by A =   _____

percent of net income used to pay credit card debt.

If C is greater than 20 percent, credit card debt may be out of control.

REVIEWING THE CREDIT CARD WORKSHEET

If you use over 20 percent of your net income to service your credit card debt, you could have a financial problem. The 20 percent figure is only an estimate and will, of course, vary among individuals. Even then, because of the high interest you pay for borrowing money, it's not wise to borrow money on credit cards.

There is no doubt that credit card debt is a financial burden, unless you pay the balance within the credit card issuer's grace period. What's more, the uncontrolled use of credit cards can push you deep into debt. Fortunately, you can do something to eliminate credit card debt.

Eliminating credit card debt

The first action you can take to eliminate credit card debt is to limit the number of credit cards you own. Most people do not need more than three or four cards. One or two cards for business and travel expenses and one or two retail cards should be enough.

Second, if you have more than one credit card loan, combine them into a new loan at a lower interest rate. The new credit card issuer will help you transfer the old balance to the new card. Third, you should consider a nonbank credit card if you have a need for the goods or services that these card companies offer. The companies that issue nonbank cards give rebates based on the use of their cards.

Finally, if you can't meet your credit card payments, don't hide from your creditors. Explain your debt problem with your creditors and try to refinance or reduce your monthly payments. After all, creditors are more interested in getting their money back than starting legal action for late payments. If you must buy with a credit card, here are some points to remember:

* Before you sign any credit card application, decide how you are going to make the payments.

* Compare the use of paying in cash and making credit card payments, be a wise shopper.

* Insist on knowing all costs before you apply for a credit card.

Solving credit problems

Why do people use credit to buy items? It would be more economical to pay cash because there wouldn't be an interest charge. There are at least two reasons most people don't pay cash. First, they are impatient. If they had to wait until they had cash to buy a car, it would probably take several years.

The second reason is that many people lack the discipline to save. Thus they go into debt, buy the car, and then in a sense engage in a negative form of savings by liquidating the debt. Usually, credit is easy to get so it takes discipline to ensure that credit payments don't get you into financial trouble.

It's always possible that an illness or the loss of your job may prevent you from paying your bills on time. If you do have a problem with your bills, try to work out a modified payment plan with your creditors. It's probably better to modify (or rebuild) your credit with the help of a financial consulting firm, bank, credit union, or another responsible party. This is viewed as the first sign of your willingness to repay your debt. The usual response from creditors is a willingness to work with you to settle the debt.

If you have a credit problem, the Consumer Credit Counseling Service (CCCS) may be able to help you. This non-profit organization with over 700 offices in 49 states will try to arrange a debt payment plan that is acceptable to you and your creditors. The CCCS also will help you set up a family expense plan at no or minimal cost. You can obtain the address of the CCCS office nearest to you by contacting:

National Foundation for Consumer Credit, Inc.
8611 Second Avenue, Suite 100
Silver Spring, MD 20910
Telephone 1-800-388-2227

Chapter 12

ESTIMATING YOUR RETIREMENT EXPENSES AND INCOME

How much time do you spend planning for retirement? If you are like many people, you devote more hours to the office Christmas party than retirement planning. With so much at stake, retirement eve is not the time to wonder if you'll have enough money to maintain your preretirement lifestyle.

Maintaining your lifestyle begins with an estimate of what your expenses will be when you retire. If you are several years from retirement, you can't accurately calculate your expenses. However, even an estimate is valuable because it gives you an idea of how much you'll need to save for a retirement free of financial worries.

In addition to your expenses, you'll need an estimate of what your income will be when you retire. This figure could vary widely, depending on what your retirement plan pays and how much you earn on investments.

If your retirement income doesn't provide enough to cover your expenses, you will have a financial problem. That means, for a comfortable retirement, you probably should save more to earn additional income.

The three worksheets that follow will help you estimate your retirement expenses and income as well as help you decide how much you should save to cover any income shortage.

RETIREMENT EXPENSES

What will your expenses be in retirement? That depends on how you want to live. Since your financial situation and expectations may change before you retire, it is difficult to predict how much you will need in retirement. You can, however, make a reasonable estimate of your expenses.

One way to estimate your expenses is to assume that you'll need 80 percent of your preretirement income to maintain your current standard of living. For example, if your preretirement income is $50,000 a year, that means you'll need $40,000.

A more accurate way is to list your current monthly expenses and estimate what they will be when you retire. When you complete the worksheet below, you'll get an idea of what your expenses will be in retirement. The figures needed for your current expenses are listed on the cash flow worksheet in Chapter 9.

RETIREMENT EXPENSES WORKSHEET

Monthly Cost Items	Current Expenses	Retirement Expenses
Mortgage/rent	$_____	$_____
Utilities (electric, gas, water, garbage, phone)	$_____	$_____
Food (grocery stores/restaurants)	$_____	$_____
Insurance (life, health, auto, housing)	$_____	$_____
Medical (not covered by insurance)	$_____	$_____
Taxes (property/income)	$_____	$_____
Auto payments	$_____	$_____
Education	$_____	$_____
Clothing	$_____	$_____
Gifts/contributions	$_____	$_____
Subscriptions (books, magazines)	$_____	$_____
Membership dues	$_____	$_____
Vacations/entertainment	$_____	$_____
Personal care	$_____	$_____
Transportation	$_____	$_____
Credit cards	$_____	$_____
Other	$_____	$_____
Totals:	$_____	$_____

Although it's difficult to predict your retirement expenses years in advance, you'll probably find that they will be less than you expect. That's because by the time you retire your house mortgage will probably be paid, you'll no longer have college expenses, groceries should be less, fewer new clothes will be needed, there will be no commuting costs to and from work, and you could possibly convert any life insurance to a paid-up policy.

RETIREMENT INCOME

After you estimate your retirement expenses, estimate your retirement income. There are five possible sources of income:
retirement plans, Social Security, savings, annuities, and investments.

One way to estimate your income is to list the income sources and total the net amounts. You can get an estimate of your retirement income from your retirement plan booklet or the retirement benefits office where you work. You can calculate Social Security benefits from the Social Security estimated monthly benefits table in Chapter 1, taking into account benefit increases. The future value of your savings, annuities, and investments you can calculate at home. Once you have the income figures, enter them on the retirement income worksheet.

RETIREMENT INCOME WORKSHEET

Monthly Income	Dollar Amount
Retirement plan at work	$_____
Social Security	$_____
Savings	$_____
Annuities	$_____
Investments	$_____
Total:	$_____
Appraisal:	
Retirement income	$_____
Minus retirement expenses	$_____
Income surplus or (shortage)	$_____

If your retirement income will be more than your expenses, you're set for a comfortable retirement. But remember, you could be retired for several years, so it's going to require not only that you have investments to supplement your income but also that they can keep pace with inflation.

On the other hand, if your expenses exceed your income, there is no doubt that you can't maintain your preretirement lifestyle. To avoid a potential shortfall, you'll need to save more money.

DECIDING HOW MUCH TO SAVE

If your retirement expenses exceed your retirement income, how much will you need to make ends meet? You can determine that by completing the required savings worksheet below. This worksheet factors the amount to save each year to cover an income shortage when you retire, and assumes a 3 percent return on your investments after adjustments for inflation and taxes. For example, let's say you'll retire in

20 years and estimate that you will need an additional $50,000 to cover your retirement expenses. In this case, you'll have to save $2,050 each year (the savings factor of .041 times $50,000) to accumulate the $50,000.

REQUIRED SAVINGS WORKSHEET

1. Income shortage $_____

2. Number of years to retirement   **Savings factor**
    5   .192
    10   .091
    15   .058
    20   .041
    25   .031
    30   .025

3. Yearly savings required
(line one times savings factor in line two) $_____

The key to a comfortable retirement is to make plans for it long before you leave your job. This involves an estimate of your retirement expenses and income, and deciding whether you'll require additional money to make ends meet.

Chapter 13

ESTATE PLANNING

There's more to retirement than just investing money and watching it grow. No matter what your age, you should have a plan for the distribution of your wealth. An estate plan will ensure that your wealth is distributed according to your wishes should anything happen to you.

Your estate is the total of all your assets, plus all that is owed to you, minus your debts. It includes your house, stocks, bonds, insurance proceeds, cash, collectibles, retirement benefits — everything you own that has a monetary value. A large part of your estate may come from your company's retirement plan, such as a 401(k), profit-sharing, or stock options.

There are two items to consider in estate planning: calculating your net worth, and providing binding instructions with the use of a will, trust, or gifts to ensure that your assets are distributed according to your wishes.

NET WORTH

The way to determine your net worth is to make a list of your assets and liabilities—a net worth statement. When you complete the net worth statement below, you'll probably find that your estate is worth more than you think, especially if you have a large equity in a home. Also, it's possible that much of your net worth is part of your personal assets. Take your furniture, for instance, which represents an investment with a dollar value. Then there is the value of any autos, boats, computers, jewelry, and paintings. In fact, anything with a dollar value you can consider an asset and include on the net worth statement.

WILLS

Regardless of the amount of your estate, you should have a will. A will is the foundation of your estate plan and the only way to ensure that your assets will pass to your beneficiaries.

NET WORTH STATEMENT

Current value		Current debt	

LIQUID ASSETS
Checking accounts $_____
Savings accounts $_____
Money market funds $_____
Insurance cash value $_____
Other liquid assets $_____

Total liquid assets $_____

LIABILITIES
Mortgages $_____
Auto loans $_____
Education loans $_____
Home equity loans $_____
Personal loans $_____
Credit card loans $_____
Other liabilities $_____

Total of all liabilities $_____

INVESTMENT ASSETS
Stocks $_____
Bonds $_____
Mutual funds $_____
Certificates of deposit $_____
Rental real estate $_____
Limited partnerships $_____
Other investments $_____
Total investment assets $_____

RETIREMENT ASSETS
IRA $_____
401(K) $_____
TSA, CODA, SEP, ESOP $_____
Profit sharing $_____
Keogh plan $_____
Defined-benefit plan $_____
Other retirement assets $_____
Total retirement assets $_____

PERSONAL ASSETS
Residence $_____
Vacation home/land $_____
Automobiles $_____
Jewelry/art/antiques $_____
Collectibles $_____
Household furnishings $_____
Computers $_____
Other personal assets $_____
Total personal assets $_____

Total of all assets $_____

Net Worth Computation
Total of all assets $_____
Minus total liabilities $_____
Your net worth $_____

If you die intestate (without a will), a court in your state will appoint someone to distribute your assets. If you are married, it would probably be your spouse. Should you be the surviving spouse, one of your children would probably be appointed. If there is no relative to distribute your assets, the court would appoint a public administrator.

The rationale underlying a will is so broad that you can do most anything you want with your assets. You can leave your assets to some of your children while excluding others. You can leave your assets to animals. You can discriminate based on race, religion, and gender. There are two broad areas where the courts could question a will. These include wills contrary to public policy and perpetual (lasting forever) wills.

Personal Representative

When you make a will, you must name a peraonal representative for your estate to carry out the terms of your will. The executor is responsible for collecting and appraising your assets, paying any due taxes, and distributing your assets to your beneficiaries. You could name your surviving spouse as the sole executor, or you can have two or more executors. For instance, you could name your spouse as the co-executor with a lawyer or bank.

Codicil

You can change your will with the use of a codicil -an addition to the original will. It's usually better to draw up a new will than have a codicil. Whether you use a codicil or write a new will, destroy the old will. An old will could be mistaken as the only will and cause problems.

Probate

Probate is a legal process that a will must pass through before assets are distributed to the beneficiaries. The executor named in the will is responsible for proving to the court that the will is valid as well as carrying out the terms of the will.

Before a will is probated, the court determines whether the will is legally written, assures that debts are paid, and oversees the proceedings of the executor until the probation process is completed. It usually takes six to ten months for a will to be probated.

You can avoid probate by keeping your assets beyond the jurisdiction of the court. This is done by transferring ownership of your assets during your lifetime. For example, you can use joint tenancy, trusts, gifts, and retirement plans to transfer assets.

JOINT TENANCY

Joint tenancy with right of survivorship is probably the easiest way to avoid probate. Any asset -a house, auto, bank account -with more than one name on the ownership document, is joint tenancy. Thus, the survivor receives title of ownership at the death of the co-owner. It's important that the ownership document state "joint tenancy with right of survivorship." Otherwise the document may have to be probated.

TRUSTS

A trust is a legal document that serves a variety of purposes for estate planning and avoiding probate. It allows you to transfer the benefits of your assets while leaving legal ownership of the assets in the trust. You could, for example, use a trust to set aside money for minor children, make gifts to charity, protect a business, or assure lifelong income for a spouse. If you create a trust, decide what you want to accomplish and then talk to a lawyer about establishing one.

Here are some other points to consider if you set up a trust:

> * You'll need to name a trustee. A trustee is responsible for administering the trust according to your instructions. Since there have been situations when an individual was the trustee and the trust's assets were stolen, it's usually better to name a bank as the trustee. If a bank employee violates the trust, presumably the bank will make restitution.

> * If you name a bank as the trustee, give your beneficiaries the power to substitute another bank. The power to change banks is important since it could protect your estate from an inefficient bank.

> * If you have minor children and you establish a living trust, you still need a simple will. This is because your minor children will need a guardian.

> * A trust should have a pour-over will to cover any assets you might forget to include in the trust. Any forgotten assets must go through probate.

There are various types of trusts designed to ensure that your assets are distributed according to your wishes. Here are some of the more common types:

Unified credit shelter trusts

This type of trust is also called a bypass trust and can be designed to provide income for a surviving spouse. It is one of the most familiar types of trusts and helps both husband and wife since each is accorded a $625,000 federal tax exemption. The surviving survivor doesn't pay taxes on the $625,000 because spouses can inherit any amount tax-free. When the surviving spouse dies the assets pass to the heirs.

To be effective, the assets in a unified credit shelter trust must be in the name of each spouse. That's because it's not known which spouse will die first. If all property is in only one name, there are no assets available to fund the bypass trust.

Qualified terminable interest property trusts (QTIPs)

A QTIP trust arranges for the trust agreement, not the spouse, to control who gets the assets at death. What happens to your estate when you die depends on what the trust specifies. A spouse could receive income from the trust, but upon the spouse's death, the principal in the trust would pass to the beneficiaries you name.

Grantor retained annuity trusts (GRATS)

Another way to pass on your estate is with a GRAT, an irrevocable trust, that lets you transfer property to the trust for a fixed number of years. It is possible, for example, to establish a GRAT on your home for your beneficiaries. What you do is place your home in trust and continue to live in it. The beneficiaries of the trust will receive the home when the trust expires. In case the beneficiaries die before the trust expires, the home is placed back into your estate.

Life insurance trusts

One way to leave tax-sheltered money to your heirs is to set up a life insurance trust to protect insurance proceeds from estate taxes. However, an insurance trust is irrevocable and you cannot get a loan on the trust's assets.

This trust works best when you purchase say, a $300,000 life insurance policy, and name someone other than yourself as trustee. You pay the yearly premiums on the insurance that are tax-sheltered and when you die the $300,000 in the trust goes to your heirs tax-free.

Charitable remainder trusts

One way to leave assets to charity and get a tax break is to set up a charitable remainder trust. In this type of trust, you receive a deduction against your estate taxes and leave some of your assets to a qualified charity.

With a charitable remainder trust, for example, you could include stocks that cost you $20,000 and increased in value to $60,000. When you set up the trust you can stipulate that a beneficiary be paid a yearly amount from the trust's income and a charitable organization control the property until the trust ends.

In the meantime, you avoid paying capital gains tax on the increased value of the stock, you get a charitable tax deduction, and the beneficiary receives income from the trust until it ends. When the trust terminates, the charity receives the property.

GIFTS

You can reduce your tax liability as much as $10,000 every year when you make tax-free gifts. A gift is the voluntary transfer of property from you to someone without any consideration of compensation. Since a spouse also is allowed the same right, a total of $20,000 can be given as gifts each year.

As you might expect, there can be problems with tax-free gifts. One difficulty, for example, is when a house is given to someone and the donor lives in it rent-free.

In this case, the IRS will consider the house part of the estate. Another area the IRS will challenge is the gift of stocks and bonds when the donor continues to receive dividends and interest income from the securities.

Gifts may play a part in reducing the tax liability of estates, but you need to plan carefully to assure they are made in compliance with IRS rules. Also, it's not wise to hand out gifts if you feel you may need the property later on.

RETIREMENT PLANS

You can include the benefits of your retirement plan in your estate. Fortunately, retirement benefits are outside the probate court's jurisdiction and pass directly to your beneficiaries.

Since much of your estate assets may come from your retirement plan, a unified credit shelter trust could protect it from federal estate taxes. To set up a unified credit shelter trust, you'll probably need to contact someone with expertise in both estate planning and retirement planning to make it work.

A Roth IRA is more than a savings vehicle for retirement. Unlike a traditional IRA, the unspent funds in a Roth IRA belong to your beneficiaries and can continue to grow tax-free over their life expectancies. Another feature of a Roth IRA is that your beneficiaries pay no income taxes on money received from a Roth. Whereas, they pay taxes on money received from a traditional IRA. However, for estate tax purposes, all IRAs, both traditional and Roth, count as part of your taxable estate.

TAXES

Types of taxes

There are three types of taxes that may be imposed because of a person's death: gift, inheritance, and estate taxes. Federal gift and estate taxes, unified under the Tax Reform Act of 1976, are imposed on the giver of property and the receiver does not pay these taxes.

Under the 1976 reform act, individuals are divided into two categories: those with estates valued under $625,000; and those over $625,000. This means that you and your spouse are allowed to make a one-time gift of $625,000 each or a total of 1.250 million tax-free to your beneficiaries. Also, your estate receives this gift even if you don't use it in your lifetime. There is no federal tax levied on estates under $625,000.

Inheritance taxes differ from estate and gift taxes in that they are imposed on the receiver of property. There are no federal inheritance taxes. However, most states have either an inheritance or estate tax and some states have both taxes. The amount of inheritance and estate taxes vary by state.

Reducing estate taxes

Fortunately, there are ways to reduce your estate taxes. You can deduct the administrative costs for handling your estate, estate debts, and bequests to charity.

Then there are martial deductions, gifts, and trusts to reduce taxes. You can leave any amount of your estate to your spouse, regardless of whether it's over or under the $625,000 exemption, and your spouse won't pay federal taxes.

Getting Professional Help

Estate planning can be difficult, so you'll probably need the services of professionals.

A lawyer can handle the legal aspects of your estate and help you determine which documents, such as wills, trusts, and gifts, would be the better way to distribute your assets. A tax accountant can help you minimize federal estate and gift taxes. And an insurance agent could review your insurance needs to protect your assets.

Part Four
SUMMARY

The surest way not to fail
is to determine to succeed.

—Sheridan

Chapter 14

GUIDELINES FOR A WEALTHY RETIREMENT

A comfortable retirement is as good as it gets. The most prosperous retirees are those who have guidelines to follow. Besides helping you make wise investments, guidelines give you the satisfaction of knowing that you are putting your plans for retirement to practical use. Here are some guidelines to consider before you invest:

SET RETIREMENT GOALS

Long before you leave your job, decide on your retirement goals. Although your goals may change as you near retirement, it's better to have them than to drift aimless toward retirement.

Your first goal is to decide when you are going to retire. Then you'll have to determine if you have enough money to live comfortably in retirement. Finally, you need an idea of what you'll do with your free time when you do retire.

PARTICIPATE IN THE RETIREMENT PLAN WHERE YOU WORK

If you are eligible, participate in the retirement plan where you work. If there's no plan at work, maybe you can open an IRA. The opportunity to gain tax-deferred or tax-free wealth is something that's hard to pass up.

UNDERSTAND YOUR RETIREMENT PLAN

It's wise to learn all you can about your retirement plan. Find out the earliest date you can retire; your investment choices; which investments could provide the highest return; the advantages of switching among investments; your vesting schedule; and the payment options that your plan provides.

BE YOUR OWN RETIREMENT PLAN MANAGER

There is a shift underway in business and government that places more responsibility for retirement on the employee's shoulders. This is seen in the move from defined-benefit retirement plans, where the employer guarantees benefits, to defined-contribution plans that puts more responsibility on the employee. The shift of responsibility means that you'll need to become more involved with your retirement plan.

HAVE AN EMERGENCY FUND

Before you invest, set aside about three months of your net pay in a money market fund or bank account for emergencies. There is no reason to hold investments if you have to sell them for emergencies.

BEFORE YOU INVEST, CHECK YOUR INSURANCE PROGRAM

It's to your advantage to have adequate life, health, accident, disability, and mortgage insurance before you invest. The amount of insurance you need depends on your age, the number and age of your dependents, and your health.

DEBT MANAGEMENT

If you have debt, don't invest until it's under control. It makes no sense to start a retirement portfolio when you have excessive debt. If you use over 20 percent of your net income for charge and credit card payments, you may have too much debt.

DIVERSIFY YOUR RETIREMENT PORTOFLIO

A diversified portfolio holds more than one investment. For instance, you could invest in mutual funds, stocks, bonds, and a money market fund. With a diversified portfolio, you lessen your risk should one type of investment not prove profitable.

BUILD YOUR PORTFOLIO GRADUALLY

Whether you have a relatively large amount to invest or only a few hundred dollars, it's usually better to move slowly when you start to invest. This requires investing bit by bit rather than a large amount at one time. For example, if you plan to put $2,000 in a mutual fund, invest the money in increments of $500 a few weeks apart.

DON'T INCLUDE TAX-FREE INVESTMENTS IN YOUR RETIREMENT PORTFOLIO

Since treasury securities, municipal bonds, and U.S. savings bonds are fully or partially tax-free, don't include them in your retirement portfolio. Tax-free investments may have a place in your overall investment plan, but there is no reason to hold them in a retirement portfolio.

Buy Only Top Performing And Pure No-Load Mutual Funds

Which are the top performing no-load mutual fund? Chapter 6,"Mutual Funds - The ideal Retirement Supplement," answers that question. Keep in mind that some funds consistently do better than others. A fund's good performance record is not a guarantee that it will perform well in the future. Yet it's a good starting point for selecting a fund.

Invest In Mutual Funds For The Long Term

When you invest in a fund, consider it a long-term investment. The big gains in funds are usually made by those who use a buy and hold strategy.

Invest Monthly In Your Mutual Funds

Mutual funds are especially attractive to people who want to invest each monthly. Moreover, if you invest all your money at one time, you stand the risk of paying too high a price for a fund. Monthly investments using the DCAP formula should provide a greater return on your money than one-time or sporadic investments in a fund. Investing monthly has another good aspect -it gets you in the habit of saving.

Reinvest Distributions

Mutual funds offer automatic reinvestment plans in which you can have dividend and capital gain distributions put back in the fund to buy additional shares. The reinvestment of distributions, a form of dollar-cost averaging, is an excellent way to increase your return on a mutual fund.

Avoid Excessive Mutual Fund Switching

It's not wise to use conversion privileges to switch in and out of funds randomly. Most studies show that trying to time the rise or fall of different funds is not as profitable as staying with one fund. The opportunity to switch funds is a useful service, but use it with discretion.

Avoid Steep Losses In Mutual Funds

Owning a treasury security guarantees that you will receive interest on your investment and your principal will be paid at maturity. Owning shares in a mutual fund has no guarantee, and there is always the chance that you will lose a large part of your investment. Although some funds carry more risk than others, you can adopt safeguards so you won't lose all of your money.

The DCAP Formula, for example, limits losses by putting a cap on the amount you invest in a fund. When you invest by the DCAP formula, you can never lose more than 25 percent of your investment. In addition, the setting and resetting of the DCAP target price will make you aware of any continuous and significant decline in the price of your fund.

You can expect a certain amount of up and down price movement with a fund, but one that drops in price and remains down for a long period may have problems. In this case, it's usually best to sell the fund.

BUY ONLY QUALITY STOCKS

Quality stocks can be found in most every industry. These stocks are industry leaders with sales and earnings that increase almost every year. They usually offer products or services with growth potential, pay dividends, and emphasize the development of new products or services. Their management is usually aggressive and experienced. These are the companies to consider if you invest in stocks.

DON'T INVEST ON TIPS, RUMORS, AND FANTASTIC PROMO-TIONS

Since the first step in making money is not to lose it, don't listen to investment tips, rumors, and "too good to be true" promotions. This is probably difficult advice to follow, yet investing on tips, rumors, and promotions is the easiest way to lose money. Always check them out before you invest.

Investors who lose about 90 percent of their money invest in promotions based on newspaper advertisements, a telephone sales pitch, or a boiler-room operation promising big profits. Most of the investors who lose money to these frauds spend almost no time investigating the organization promoting the investment or the risks involved.

SET A LOSS LIMIT ON STOCKS

Before you invest in a stock, set a limit on the loss you will tolerate should it drop in price. If you buy a stock at $20, for example, limit any loss to 10 percent. In this case, you would sell the stock if it drops to $18. When you limit losses, it leaves most of your money available to buy another stock that may prove profitable.

USE LEVERAGE WITH CARE

If you use leverage (borrow money from a broker) to invest in stocks, use it sparingly. It's true that you could double your profits, but you also could double your losses. What's more, if you use leverage and your stocks drop in price, your broker may ask that you add money to your account.

DON'T GET INVOLVED IN SHORT SELLING, OPTIONS, AND COMMODITIES

Short selling, options, and commodities investments are risky, so it's usually better to avoid them. Few people consistently make money with short selling, options, or commodities.

Be Careful With Individual Bonds

If you buy municipal or corporate bonds, consider a bond mutual fund. Buying individual bonds, especially those that are not quality-grade, can be risky. When you invest in a bond fund, your risk is reduced because you own a part of several bonds as opposed to a single bond that could drop significantly in price or even default on its interest payments.

Avoid Investments In Gold, Silver, Art, And Collectibles

Investments in precious metals, art, and collectibles carry a large amount of risk. Many people tout them as a hedge against inflation, but there are other investments with less risk that can provide the same hedge.

Save On Taxes

No one wants to pay more taxes than the law requires, yet many people do. Here are ways to save on taxes:

* Invest the maximum in your company's retirement plan.

* Invest in a Keogh or SEP if you have self-employment income.

* Shift income to a child who is in a lower tax bracket.

* Take out a tax-deductible home equity loan to pay off auto and credit card debt.

* Donate to a charity to get a tax deduction.

* Set up a trust to save on estate taxes.

It's to your advantage to set some guidelines when you invest. They don't have to be complex —just basic rules to follow. As you gain investing experience, you'll probably add more guidelines to the above list. The important point is to have guidelines and to stick with them.

Chapter 15

Questions And Answers About Retirement

The purpose of this book is to share information with you that will help you retire wealthy. The book is neither a "crash course" for retirement nor does it cover all aspects of retirement. Rather, the book shows how it is possible to retire wealthy if you have a sound retirement program and avoid costly mistakes.

The following are questions and answers that you may have about the topics covered in this book. It's possible that some of your questions may go unanswered. If so, contact the employee benefits representative where you work, a mutual fund salesperson, or your financial planner.

Q: Are there many workers who don't have a retirement plan?
A: Although about 40 million workers have some type of employer sponsored retirement plan, some 50 percent of the full-time work force has no retirement coverage other than Social Security.

Q: Why are there so many workers without a retirement plan?
A: There are several reasons. First, the government's reluctance to provide enough incentives for workers to contribute to a plan; second, employer indifference about starting a plan for their employees; and finally, the lack of awareness that many employees have about the benefits of a retirement plan.

Q: In recent years, what are the most significant changes that have occurred in retirement planning?
A: One important change has been an increase in the number of employers offering defined-contribution retirement plans and a decrease in the number of defined-benefit plans. A defined- contribution plan provides a range of investments, but it also

places more responsibility on workers for their retirement.Another change has been the creation of the Roth IRA: The Roth IRA has many features that can help you accumulate a larger retirement nest egg.

Q: How long before I retire should I apply for Social Security benefits?
A: It's a good idea to apply for Social Security benefits about three months before you retire. This way you can be sure that you'll begin receiving checks the month you actually retire.

Q: How does Social Security determine benefits for disability?
A: To be eligible for disability benefits under Social Security, you must have worked long enough and recently enough to qualify. You can earn up to four credits each year you work. The number of work credits needed for disability depends on your age and when you become disabled. In addition, family members who qualify for benefits on your record do not need work credits.

Remember, Social Security has a strict definition of disability. Even though you can't perform your job, that doesn't mean you'll qualify for disability benefits. For example, maybe you can't continue your job as a test pilot because of a back injury, but you probably could dispense "Big Macs".

Q: I plan to become self-employed in a couple of years. Will I have to pay Social Security taxes on my earnings?
A: When you become self-employed, you'll have to pay an earnings tax of 15.3 percent. The tax includes 12.4 percent for Social Security and 2.9 percent for Medicare. If you want more information on Social Security and self-employment taxes, call 1-800-772-1213 and ask for publication no. 05-10022.

Q: When I begin drawing Social Security benefits, will I have to pay taxes on the money I receive?
A: Yes, if your income exceeds certain levels. For example, if you are unmarried with income over $34,000 or married earning over $44,000, 85 percent of your Social Security benefits will be taxable.

Q: Can anyone contribute to an IRA?
A: Yes, as long as the person works and earns an income. Income for IRA purposes includes wages, bonuses, professional fees, commissions, tips, and other kinds of income. Even legally separated and divorced people receiving child support or alimony may contribute to an IRA:

Q: What is the difference between a deductible and nondeductible IRA?
A: With a deductible IRA, contributions are deducted from your income and tax-deferred until you begin withdrawals. Nondeductible IRA contributions are also tax-deferred until withdrawals begin, but they are not deductible from your income.

Q: Is it possible to withdraw money from my IRA before age 59 and 1/2 and not pay a penalty and taxes?
A: If you are disabled, you can receive your IRA money before the regular withdrawal age of 59 and 1/2 and not pay a penalty and taxes.Another way to avoid a penalty and taxes is to make annual withdrawals designed to exhaust your IRA during your lifetime. However, this method may not furnish much income if you've only contributed to your IRA for a few years. If possible, it's better to wait until age 59 and 1/2 when withdrawals should provide more money.

Q: Where can I open an IRA and is there a charge for opening one?
A: You can open an IRA with a mutual fund, brokerage house, bank, credit union, or insurance company. The cost is typically $25 to open an IRA account and $25 a year for maintenance.

Q: Can I move my IRA account from one trustee to another at any time?
A: Your IRA account can be moved at any time and as often as you like from one IRA trustee to another. However, if you take possession of your IRA money and then reinvest it with another trustee, you can only do this once a year. Also, if you receive your IRA money, it has to be reinvested within 60 days or you're subject to a withdrawal penalty and taxes.
If you plan to move your IRA, the best way is to transfer your account from one trustee to another and not worry about a penalty and taxes.

Q: What is a rollover IRA?
A: It's a command that I give to my dog. Seriously, it's a way to transfer money from one qualified retirement plan to an IRA to defer taxes. It's also called a tax-free rollover. You can rollover all or part of your retirement plan into an IRA:

Q: If I rollover my traditional IRA to a Roth IRA, will I have to pay a penalty?
A: There is no penalty to rollover a traditional IRA to a Roth IRA:

Q: Can I received a distribution from a Roth IRA before I'd held it five years?
A: Yes, but you would be required to pay taxes and a 10 percent penalty on the earnings, unless you meet an exception to the penalty tax.

Q: Can I rollover my 401(K) or other qualified retirement plan into a Roth IRA?
A: No. The current rules only allow you to rollover the money into a traditional IRA:

Q: When I retire, how will my traditional IRA distributions be taxed?
A: You won't pay taxes on your nondeductible contributions, but you must pay regular income taxes on your deductible contributions.

Q: Do you have an IRA? If so, what type is it?
A: I have a self-directed, traditional IRA:

Q: Who is the trustee for your IRA?
A: Charles Schwab, a discount brokerage firm, is the trustee.

Q: Why do I have to wait until I'm age 59 and 1/2 to begin regular withdrawals from an IRA? Why not age 55 or even 50?
A: The answer to your question is interesting. It's because the age for regular withdrawals came from the Keogh plan. It was introduced in the Keogh because 59 and 1/2 is the midpoint age of many company retirement plans at 55 and Social Security's age of 65 for full benefits.

Q: Where can I get more information about IRAs?
A: Contact the IRS and request a copy of Publication 590, Individual Retirement Arrangements.

Q: How does the Pension Benefit Guaranty Corporation (PBGC) insure the retirement benefits of workers?
A: The PBGC guarantees the benefits of defined-benefit pension plans, similar to the way FDIC insures bank deposits. PBGC is funded by the sponsors of defined-benefit plans who pay a premium per employee for coverage. When underfunded plans cannot meet their obligations, workers can receive a monthly benefit from the PBGC. The PBGC also pays a spousal survivor benefit that must be at least one-half of the employee's benefit.

Q: My employer contributes an amount equal to 5 percent of my salary to my 401(K). Can I also contribute to the plan?
A: That depends on the rules of your employer's 401(K). If the plan allows employee participation, you can contribute. In 1998, if allowed, you could contribute up to $10,000 of your salary.

Q: If I put the maximum the rules allow into a 401(K), can I still contribute to a traditional IRA?
A: Yes. Moreover, your IRA contribution will be fully tax-deductible if you are single and your adjusted gross income doesn't exceed $25,000 or $40,000 if you are married.

Q: Do you think it's a wise idea to borrow from my 401(K) to pay off my credit card debt?
A: Only if you have no other options. Your 401(K) is for your retirement and you shouldn't put that at risk. A better option is to increase your monthly credit card payments.

Q: Is the DCAP formula a good way to invest in an IRA?

A: It's an excellent way to invest in an IRA and here's how to do it. Let's say you plan to put $2,000 in an IRA every year and your investment money is available on January 2. On that date, invest all of your $2,000 in a IRA money market fund so interest can start compounding tax-deferred. Next, open an account with a mutual fund and satisfy the initial investment requirement. Finally, invest the remainder of your $2,000 in your mutual fund during the year according to the DCAP formula.

Q: Which of the retirement plans is the best one?

A: Probably the 403(b) -the tax-sheltered annuity (TSA). That's because you can generally save more with it than most other plans. You can contribute up to $9,500 of your income each year. If your employer also contributes to your TSA, the combined contributions cannot exceed more than 25 percent of your income or $30,000. However, to be eligible for a TSA, you have to be an employee of a public school or tax-exempt organization, so that limits the number of participants.

Q: Is it possible for me to transfer from one TSA to another?

A: Yes, but let the trustee of your TSA handle the transaction so you will avoid a penalty and taxes.

Q: Can I leave my TSA with my old employer if I accept a new job?

A: You can request that your TSA remain with your old employer, but the account is frozen and you cannot continue making
contributions to it. You could rollover your TSA into your new employer's retirement plan, or to an IRA:

Q: Can I contribute to my TSA as well as an IRA?

A: You can contribute to any qualified retirement plan including your TSA and still contribute to an IRA, if you meet the eligibility requirements.

Q: I work for a state government and I'm required to contribute 5 percent of my gross income to my retirement plan. Can a state deduct 5 percent from my salary and put the money in a retirement plan, even when I don't want to contribute?

A: State governments, as well as the federal government, can require you and their other employees to contribute to a retirement plan. It's to your benefit to contribute to the plan. Take advantage of it.

Q: I'm an employer with only a few workers, and I want to start a retirement plan for them. Do you think a SEP is the right type of plan?

A: A SEP is a good plan for small employers. This is because it provides retirement benefits without the high start-up and operating costs of other types of plans. Usually, SEP contributions are made by employers, not employees. With a SEP, your contributions are tax-deductible, your business pays no taxes on the earnings of SEP investments, there is no obligation for you to make contributions every year, and a financial institution can handle the SEP money, which relieves you of many management responsibilities.

Q: Do you think a revocable trust is a good idea?
A: There are pros and cons about the value of a revocable trust. A revocable trust has management headaches and expenses and it may not provide any tax savings. However, it will avoid probate and the time beneficiaries will have to wait to inherit an estate.

Q: If I receive $10,000 as a gift from someone, how do I report it on my income taxes? Or is it exempt from gift taxes?
A: The gift is not taxable, so you would not report it on your income tax return.

Q: What is the major problem that most people face in retirement? And what can I do to ease the transition from work to retirement?
A: The biggest problem retirees probably face is establishing a new sense of identity. That's because many people are so involved with their work there is a loss of status and recognition when they retire.

The way to soften the move from work to retirement is to retire to something. Do something you enjoy. What you do doesn't have to be a full-time job, but anything, even a hobby, part-time job, volunteer work — something that interests you. Remember, you can't enjoy rabbit stew without a rabbit, and most people can't enjoy retirement without something to do.

Q: If I receive an early retirement offer, what's the first thing to consider?
A: With an early retirement offer, you'll first have to determine if you can live off the reduced income. Maybe you'll have to wait for full retirement when your benefits will be more.

Another consideration is that many people underestimate what it will cost to maintain their preretirement living standard. This is especially true if you live 20 or 30 years after you retire. That's why it's important to have an investment portfolio to supplement your retirement income.

Q: How long before I retire should I decide whether I'll have enough to cover my retirement expenses?
A: Before you decide whether you'll have enough to live on in retirement, you need at least an idea of when you'll retire. Once you know that, no later than ten years before your expected retirement date, determine whether you'll earn enough to cover your expenses. If you won't have enough, you'll have to save more money to make ends meet.

Your living expenses in retirement should be about 80 percent of the income you earned just before you retire. If you like to travel frequently or you have high medical expenses, the 80 percent figure may be too low. Some of your costs in retirement will decrease, but others may increase so you'll have to be objective when you determine your expenses.

Q: If my retirement expenses are more than my income, what's the best way to earn extra money?
A: Before you retire, take an inventory of your assets. It's possible that you could sell some of your assets to provide more income. For example, you could sell your house and buy a less expensive one or rent an apartment to cut costs, or you could sell some of your art, antiques, or collectibles for extra income.

Q: I'd like to know how long you have been an investor in mutual funds, if you also invest in stocks, and how successful you have been using the DCAP formula?
A: I've been an investor in mutual funds for about twenty years and in stocks for about thirty-five years. I've had a fair amount of success with stocks, but I have had even more success investing in mutual funds. I have used the DCAP formula to invest in mutual funds for about six years. I wish I had developed the formula earlier, when I started investing. If I had, I'd be richer now.

Q: I'm intrigued with the DCAP formula. Does it really work?
A: The DCAP formula has worked beautifully for me. Let me give you an example of the formula's success. Since 1993, when I began using the formula to invest in the CGM Capital Development Fund, my average annual return has been about 22 percent. The return includes the reinvestment of all dividend and capital gain distributions to buy additional shares. That certainly beats the CD rate of around 6 percent. But remember, there is no guarantee that your return will be 22 percent when you invest by the formula.

Q: Will you explain how the formula works if a fund's price drops below the target price?
A: After I make my initial investment in a fund, I set the target price that determines the amount of future investments. If the fund's price, its net asset value, drops below the target price, I increase the amount of my investment. For example, should the fund's price drop 5 percent below the target price, I increase my investment 20 percent. A 10 percent drop, requires an increase of 40 percent. Thus, if my minimum investment is $100 and the fund's price drops 25 percent below the target price, my monthly investment increases to $200. Each 5 percent drop in the fund's price requires that I increase my investment 20 percent, but only to a total of 100 percent.

The 5 percent figure also works in reverse. For example, let's say my fund drops 25 percent from its target price and then goes up in price. In this case, for each 5 percent increase in the fund's price toward the target price, my investments decrease 20 percent to a total of 100 percent.

Q: How much luck is involved when you invest in a fund or a stock and its price goes up?
A: I have no idea, but I do know the harder I work the luckier I get.

Q: Do you use the DCAP formula when you invest in stocks?
A: Not yet, although I have bought stocks and averaged down. That is, when the price of the stocks dropped, I purchased more shares to lower my average cost per share. This is similar to using the formula. I am experimenting with the formula to invest in stocks, but I feel it may have to be revised to accommodate them.

Q: Where do you get the information you need to invest in stocks?
A: I watch the stock market ticker tapes on television; receive stock charts on my computer from TeleChart 2000; and subscribe to *Forbes, Investor's Business Daily, Mutual Funds,* and *Smart Money.*

Q: There are several publications that tout switching from one fund to another for greater profits. Do you advise switching in and out of funds?
A: Trust everyone, but always cut the cards. That means listen to the sales pitch of these publications but do your homework before you invest in a fund. The way to make big bucks in funds is to research several funds, select one with a good performance record, and invest for the long term using the DCAP formula.

Q: I've noticed that many funds advertise about the number of "stars" given to them by fund rating services. What's the significance of these stars?
A: Supposedly, the more stars the better a fund will perform. Unfortunately, the "star wars" ranking of mutual funds has become a fad. I don't place too much importance on these rankings because some rating services give stars to every fund, even the worst performers. I avoid the "star wars" craze and do my own rankings based on the performance of a fund over a number of years.

Q: I assume that you don't approve of timing mutual fund investments and frequent switching among funds?
A: Yes and no. If you have a relatively large amount to invest in December, I'd wait until the next year. That's because most mutual funds make distributions in December, so you'd immediately have to pay taxes on your investment.

It should come as no surprise, however, that a few investors switch their mutual fund accounts to money market funds before a distribution to avoid taxes. After the distribution, the withdrawn money is then reinvested in the same or another fund.

If you use a buy and hold strategy rather than switching funds, I think you'll receive a better return. Most studies show that frequent switching among funds is not as profitable as sticking with one fund.

Q: What is the most important item to consider when I screen mutual funds for investment purposes?
A: By far, the most important selection criteria is the fund's past performance in both up and down market cycles.

Q: How can I get information on the fees that funds charge?
A: Since a fund must disclose all its fees in its prospectus, that's where to get the information. Remember, funds can impose front-end loads, 12b-1 fees, back-end loads, and management and customer service fees. Not all of these fees are assessed by most funds, but in recent years there has been an increase in the amount and number of fees. When you receive a prospectus, add up the different fees and use this as a reference when comparing funds.

Q: What if I need more information than I can find in a fund's prospectus?
A: Ask the fund for its Statement of Additional Information (SAI). Funds must provide this statement free of charge to anyone who requests it. The SAI includes: a list of the securities in the fund at the end of the fund's fiscal year; a record of the fund's officers and directors, including their occupation and the pay they receive from the fund; information about anyone who owns more than 5 percent of the fund's shares; and the fund's financial statement.

Q: I want to invest in a mutual fund, but I really don't have the nerve to do it. Do you have any suggestions on how I can reduce my nervousness and begin investing in a fund?
A: If you're nervous about investing in funds, do your homework. Go to the library and read about mutual funds. Get the telephone number of some funds and call for a prospectus. Compare the average return, fees, services, and objectives of several funds. On the basis of your comparison, select the fund that has the highest return and meets your investment objectives. After you have invested in the fund for a couple of years, look at its total return. Compare the return with what you could have earned with similar investments. If you selected a good fund, you'll probably find that the fund earned more than other investments and your nervousness has disappeared. Once you are comfortable with one fund, start investing in other funds to diversify your portfolio.

Q: What is the most important thing to consider when I screen funds for investment purposes, and what is a good return for a fund?
A: By far, the most important screening item is the fund's past performance in both up and down market cycles. Generally, the more years you check a fund's performance the better you can predict its future return. A good annual return for a fund is 15 percent or better since its inception.

Q: What are asset allocation funds?
A: These are funds that invest in U.S. stocks, bonds, metals, foreign stocks -almost anything. They are especially attractive to investors who can't decide how to allocate their money among funds with different objectives, and those who believe that different types of investments reduce risk.

You could duplicate an asset allocation fund by investing in several types of funds, but this would involve screening many funds to select those that meet your investment objectives. So asset allocation funds do simplify the selection process. In addition, fees and commissions are less when you invest in one rather than several funds.

Q: I have a CD that's about to mature and my bank wants me to invest the money in a mutual fund it sponsors. Do you think this is a good idea, and are the funds sold by banks insured by the FDIC?
A: No, to both of your questions. Since banks only sell load mutual funds, avoid funds sold by banks. Also, none of the over 7,000 mutual funds are insured by the FDIC, including those sold by banks.

Glossary Of Terms

Account: A bookkeeping record of a client's transactions with an investment firm. It includes a client's credit and debit balances of cash and securities.

Accrued benefits: The accumulation of pension credits for years of work in a company's defined-benefit plan. In a defined-contribution plan, the accumulation of funds in a retirement account.

Actuary: A professional person who calculates statistical risks, premiums, life expectancies, and makes analyses for insurance companies.

Adjusted gross income (AGI): The total income as reported on a tax return less items allowed as adjustments.

Annuitant: A person who receives benefits from an annuity.

Annuity: An investment contract sold by a life insurance company that promises payment over a specified period.

Ask price: The net asset value (NAV) plus any sales charge of a mutual fund.

Asset: Any item of value owned by an individual or corporation.

Asset allocation: Dividing a portfolio among several investments that are affected by different degrees of risk and economic conditions.

Automatic monthly investment: An optional contractual plan for investing in mutual funds. The investor makes payments to a fund on a monthly, quarterly, or other basis.

Automatic reinvestment plan (ARP): An option available to mutual fund shareholders by which their dividends and capital gains are reinvested to buy additional shares.

Automatic withdrawal: An option available to mutual fund shareholders that allows them to receive a fixed dollar amount of their assets periodically.

Average annual total return: The total of a mutual fund's price increase or decrease plus distributions for one year. Expressed as a percentage of increase or decrease.

Back-end load: A fee charged by a mutual fund when a shareholder redeems shares. Also called redemption fee or deferred sales charge.

Balanced fund: A mutual fund with two objectives: current income and long-term capital gains.

Banker's acceptance: A short-term, non-interest bearing note sold at discount and redeemed at full value.

Bear market: A period when stock prices are going down, usually for an extended period of time; the opposite of a bull market.

Beneficiary: The person designated to receive property from a will, trust, insurance policy, or retirement plan.

Bond: A debt security in the form of a loan that obligates the issuer to pay interest and repay the bondholder the face amount at maturity.

Bond fund: A collection of bonds issued by several corporations with varying maturity dates and managed by an investment company.

Break in service: A calendar year, retirement plan year, or other 12-month period when a participant in a retirement plan does not work more than 499 hours for an employer.

Broker (stockbroker): A person or firm that acts as an intermediary between buyers and sellers of securities.

Bull market: A period when stock prices are going up, usually for an extended period of time; the opposite of a bear market.

Buy-back: The right of a terminated employee who was less than 50 percent vested to buy back forfeited benefits.

Capital appreciation: An increase in the value of an asset such as stocks, bonds, mutual funds, and other types of investments. Also called appreciation.

Capital gain: The profit from the sale of an asset.

Capital loss: The loss from the sale of an asset.

Cash flow: The movement of money into and from a financial account.

Cash-out: A lump-sum payment of an employee's nonforfeitable pension account prior to retirement.

Certificate of deposit (CD): A certificate issued for money deposited in a bank or savings and loan association for a specified period of time at a specific rate of interest.

Charitable remainder trust: A trust that leaves assets to a charity at a future date. The grantor usually receives income from the trust while living, but upon the grantor's death the principal belongs to the charity.

Cliff vesting: A method to calculate when employees are entitled to an employer's contribution to their retirement plan. Full benefits are awarded after a maximum of five years of qualifying employment with a company.

Closed-end fund: A managed investment fund with a fixed number of shares traded in the securities markets through brokers.

Codicil: Amendments to a will.

Collateral: An asset used to secure a loan. If the loan is not repaid, the asset may be seized.

Commercial paper: Unsecured promissory notes issued by corporations to provide them with short-term financing.

Commission: A fee charged by a broker for buying and selling securities for an individual or investment firm.

Common stock: Securities that represent ownership in a company, issued in units of shares.

Compound interest: Interest paid on both the principal (face amount) and the unpaid accrued interest.

Consumer Price Index (CPI): A rate computed by the government to measure the increase or decrease in the cost of goods and services during a specified period.

Conversion privilege: The right of a mutual fund shareholder to switch from one fund to another.

Corporation (company): A business organization chartered by a state to conduct business within the state.

Cost-of-Living Adjustment (COLA): An annual adjustment in wage or retirement benefits that reflects changes in the Consumer Price Index (CPI).

Custodian (trustee): An organization that holds investments for safekeeping. See fiduciary.

Default: The failure of a company to make bond or loan payments when due.

Defined-benefit plan: A pension plan paid for by the employer and guaranteed by the Pension Benefit Guaranty Corporation. A defined-benefit plan pays a fixed amount to qualified employees at retirement.

Defined-contribution plan: An employer sponsored plan that pays retirement benefits to qualified employees. The benefit amount is based on the performance of investments in the plan.

Discount broker: A brokerage firm that handles customer buy and sell orders and charges lower commissions than a full-service broker. See full-service broker.

Distributions: Dividends and capital gains paid to mutual fund shareholders.

Diversification: A method of investing that involves buying several types of securities to reduce risk.

Dividend: A payment by a company in the form of cash, stock, or assets to its shareholders.

Dividend reinvestment plan: See automatic reinvestment plan (ARP).

Dollar-cost averaging: A method for investing equal amounts at regular intervals.

Dollar-Cost Averaging Plus (DCAP):. A formula for investing varying amounts in an open-end mutual fund.

Dow Jones Averages: A measure of stock market price movement based on thirty industrial, twenty transportation, and fifteen utility stocks.

Early retirement: Retirement before a company's normal retirement age. An employee that retires early may receive an immediate but reduced pension.

Earnings per share: The net income of a company based on the total shares outstanding; computed by dividing the shares outstanding by the net earnings.

Employee Stock Ownership Plan (ESOP):A plan that allows qualified employees to share ownership in a company. Employee ownership is acquired through the contribution of company stock by the employer.

Employment Retirement Income Security Act (ERISA): The federal law that created standards for establishing and maintaining corporate pension plans.

Equities: Stocks, real estate, and other assets that an investor owns, but not bonds since an investor lends money for their purchase.

Estate: 1. All real and personal property in which a person has an interest. 2. The assets and liabilities left by a person at death.

Estate tax: Tax levied on the estate of a deceased person.

Face value: 1. The death benefit amount of a life insurance policy. 2. The amount of a bond that the issuer promises to repay.

Family of funds: A group of mutual funds, each having a different objective, but managed by the same investment company. A family usually consists of stock, bond, and money market funds.

Federal Insurance Contributions Act (FICA): Federal Act that taxes workers and provides them with Social Security and Medicare benefits.

Fiduciary: A corporation or person entrusted with the control of assets for the benefit of others. See trustee.

401(K): A tax-deferred employee retirement plan provided by an employer.

Front-end load: A sales charge that investors pay when buying shares of some mutual funds. See load fund.

Full-service broker: A broker who handles buy and sell orders, research, and other services for clients. See discount broker.

Gift: The transfer of assets from one person to another person or to an organization.

Gift tax exemption: The right that allows a person to give cash or assets, up to $10,000 annually, to an unlimited number of people.

Government securities: A generic name for U.S. Government securities which include treasury bills, notes, and bonds; Series EE and HH Bonds; certificates of indebtedness for interbank and interagency transfers of funds; and agency securities such as Federal National Mortgage Association (FNMA) and Government National Mortgage Association (GNMA).

Graded vesting: A vesting schedule where an employee is partially vested, typically 25 percent, after a specific number of work years. The vesting schedule increases until full vesting is achieved.

Grantor: The person who creates a trust.

Grantor retained annuity trust (GRAT): An irrevocable trust that allows the transfer of property to the trust for a specified number of years to avoid estate taxes.

Growth and income fund: A mutual fund that invests in the common stock of established companies that have increasing share value and a record of paying relatively high dividends.

Growth fund: A mutual fund that invests primarily in the common stock of companies whose sales and earnings are expanding. These funds tend to hold stocks that are expected to increase in value as opposed to those that pay a relatively high dividend.

Growth stock: The common stock of a company whose sales and earnings are increasing in value at a relatively rapid rate.

Guaranteed investment contract (GIC): A fixed income investment, similar to a CD, purchased from insurance companies for inclusion in a retirement plan.

Heir: A person who legally inherits or is entitled to inherit the property of someone who died.

Index: A measure of stock market movement. Examples are Dow-Jones Industrial Average, Standard and Poor's 500, and NASDAQ Index.

Individual Retirement Account (IRA): A tax-deferred retirement account for employed persons and their spouses.

Inflation: An increase in the selling cost of goods and services resulting in a decrease of what a dollar will buy of these goods and services.

Interest: Money paid to a lender by a borrower for the use of the money.

Interest rate: The rate of payment, expressed as a percentage, to the lender of money by a borrower of the money.

Intestate: Status of a person who dies without a will.

Investment advisor: A person or organization that provides advice on investments for a fee.

Investment company: A corporation, trust or partnership that invests the pooled money of shareholders in securities according to investment objectives. A mutual fund is an investment company.

Investment objective: The goal of an individual or investment company.

Joint tenancy (with right of survivorship): Joint control over property by two or more people. When one tenant dies, property goes to surviving tenant(s).

Keogh Plan: A retirement investment plan for self-employed persons.

Leverage: The use of borrowed money, usually from a brokerage firm, to purchase stocks and other types of investments.

Life insurance trust: The disposition of life insurance proceeds through the use of a trust.

Liquid asset: An investment that can be converted to cash easily, preferably without losing its value.

Living trust: An inter vivos trust that is effective during the holder's lifetime. It does not pass through probate when the holder dies.

Load fund: A mutual fund that charges a fee when shares are purchased in the fund. See no-load mutual fund.

Lumpsum: The one-time payment of an entire retirement account within a calendar year.

Management company: An investment company that directs the operations of a mutual fund; also called an investment adviser.

Maturity date: A specific date when the borrower of money is required to repay the principal amount of a debt.

Medicaid: A federal/state funded health care program for people with low or no income.

Medicare: Federal health insurance program for qualified persons age 65 and older.

Money market mutual fund: A fund that invests in short-term securities such as certificates of deposit, commercial paper, government securities, and bankers' acceptances.

Municipal bond fund: An open-end mutual fund or unit trust that invests in tax-exempt bonds issued by state, city, and local governments.

Mutual fund: An investment company that pools money from investors so that it can be more conveniently, economically, and efficiently managed and invested in securities.

NASDAQ: Acronym for the National Association of Security Dealers Automated Quotations. NASDAQ provides price and volume figures on securities traded on the over-the-counter market.

Net asset value (NAV): The price per share of a mutual fund, determined by dividing the number of shares outstanding into the net assets of a fund.

Net worth: The total assets of an individual or company less the total of all liabilities.

New York Stock Exchange (NYSE): The largest and oldest stock exchange in the United States. Generally, the shares traded on the NYSE are those of larger companies.

No-load mutual fund: A mutual fund that does not have a sales charge, such as a front-end load. See also load fund.

Open-end fund: A managed investment company (mutual fund) that does not have a fixed number of shares. Shares of open-end companies are sold and redeemed on investor's demand.

Over-the-counter: A market where securities that are not traded on any exchange, such as the New York Stock Exchange, are bought and sold at bid and ask prices.

Participant: A person taking part in, eligible to receive benefits from, or receiving benefits from a retirement plan.

Payment date: The date when either a stock dividend or bond interest will be paid by the issuer.

Payout: The method an employer uses to distribute retirement benefits.

Periodic payment plan: A contractual plan for investing in mutual funds. The investor makes payments to a fund on a monthly, quarterly, or other basis for a specified number of years.

Personal Representative: A person or organization designated to carry out the provisions and directions in a will.

Portfolio: The total investment holdings of an individual or an investment company.

Portfolio manager: Professional mutual fund or other investment company manager who makes buy and sell decisions on securities according to stated objectives.

Price range: The high and low prices of a security or mutual fund for a specified period, often called a trading range.

Probate: The court process that a will must pass through before assets can be distributed to beneficiaries.

Profit-sharing plan: A plan set up by an employer that provides for the sharing of company profits with employees or their beneficiaries.

Prospectus: The official booklet required by the Securities and Exchange Commission that describes a mutual fund's objectives, policies, restrictions, and other information.

Pure no-load mutual fund: A mutual fund that does not have a front-end load, back-end load, or a 12b-1 fee.

Qualified retirement plan: A pension or retirement plan designed to be exempt from taxes until money is withdrawn.

Qualified terminable interest property (QTIP) trust: A trust designed so the grantor, not the spouse, can choose the beneficiary.

Rate of return: The gain or loss on an investment, expressed as a percentage.

Redemption fee: See back-end load.

Reinvestment privilege: See automatic reinvestment plan (ARP).

Return on investment (yield): The percentage gain or loss on an investment.

Revocable trust: A trust in which the owner has control of the assets.

Risk: The chance that all or part of a person's investment money will be lost.

Rollover (tax-free): The tax-free transfer of assets from one qualified retirement plan to another qualified retirement plan.

Sales charge: A commission charged to invest in mutual funds, unit trusts, limited partnerships, and other investments.

Securities: Stocks, bonds, warrants, options, and other investments.

Securities and Exchange Commission (SEC): The federal agency established to protect investors.

Shareholder: A person or legal entity that owns common or preferred stock in a corporation, or shares in a mutual fund.

Simplified Employee Pension (SEP): A retirement plan for employer contributions to an employee's IRA. Also a retirement plan for self-employed persons. A SEP is both a pension and a type of IRA.

Social Security Administration (SSA): The government agency that administers the Social Security programs.

Standard and Poor's (S&P) 500: A measure of the value change of 500 common stocks. The S&P 500 is used as a comparison for stock market performance.

Statement of additional information (SAI): A report provided by mutual funds that contains more information than what is included in a fund's prospectus.

Successor trustee: Person or organization named for managing a trust if the first trustee cannot fulfill the trust's obligations.

Summary plan description: A booklet that explains the main features of an employee's retirement plan. Required by ERISA for all pension plans.

Switching (mutual funds): See conversion privilege.

Target-Benefit Plan: A defined-benefit retirement plan that uses a target amount to set a participant's benefits that are paid by the employer. The employer does not guarantee that the target benefit will be achieved.

Target price: An arbitrary price set by mutual fund shareholders to calculate the amount of monthly investments when using the DCAP formula.

Tax-deferred: The delayed payment of a tax liability on retirement plans such as IRAs, 401(Ks), and certain annuities.

Tax-exempt securities: Generally refers to municipal bonds issued by state, city, and local governments.

Tax rate: The percentage of an individual's or company's income subject to taxes.

Tax-shelter: An investment that reduces or defers taxable income.

Tax-Sheltered Annuity (TSA): A retirement plan established under Section 403(b) of Internal Revenue Code for employees of public schools and tax-exempt organizations.

Thrift Savings Plan: A defined-contribution retirement plan for employees of the federal government.

Total return: A performance calculation that includes the change in an investment's value plus any payment of dividends and capital gains, expressed as a percentage.

Transactions: The buying and selling of securities.

Trust: A legal relationship that transfers the ownership of property to a trustee who is responsible for retaining the property for the trust's beneficiaries.

Trustee: The person or organization holding title to trust property for the purposes stated in the terms of the trust. Also an organization that holds investments for safe-keeping.

12b-1 fee: A charge that some mutual funds assess to cover marketing and distribution costs.

Unified credit shelter trust: Actually a will divided in two parts. Part of the assets go to the spouse and part to other beneficiaries. Also called a bypass trust.

Vestin:. The period of time an employee must work to receive the benefits accrued in a retirement plan.

Volatility: The measure of a security's or stock market's price movement.

Will: A legal document that distributes a person's property at death.

Year of service: A 12-month period in which an employee works a specific number of hours or equivalent. Used to determine eligibility for participation in a retirement plan, vesting, and accrued benefits.

Yield: Income on an investment expressed as a percentage.

Zero-coupon bond: A debt security issued at a discount from its face value. No actual interest is paid until the bond matures.

Zero-coupon bond fund: A mutual fund that invests in debt securities issued by the government, a municipality, or corporation, bought at a discount from their face value.

Index

INDEX